DIGITAL MARKETING
AN OVERVIEW

DR. ANTONY PUTHUSSERY

INDIA • SINGAPORE • MALAYSIA

Notion Press

Old No. 38, New No. 6
McNichols Road, Chetpet
Chennai - 600 031

First Published by Notion Press 2020
Copyright © Dr. Antony Puthussery 2020
All Rights Reserved.

ISBN
Hardcase 978-1-64828-830-2
Paperback 978-1-64783-866-9

This book has been published with all efforts taken to make the material error-free after the consent of the author. However, the author and the publisher do not assume and hereby disclaim any liability to any party for any loss, damage, or disruption caused by errors or omissions, whether such errors or omissions result from negligence, accident, or any other cause.

While every effort has been made to avoid any mistake or omission, this publication is being sold on the condition and understanding that neither the author nor the publishers or printers would be liable in any manner to any person by reason of any mistake or omission in this publication or for any action taken or omitted to be taken or advice rendered or accepted on the basis of this work. For any defect in printing or binding the publishers will be liable only to replace the defective copy by another copy of this work then available.

CONTENTS

Chapter – 1	Introduction to Digital Marketing	5
Chapter – 2	Facebook Marketing	24
Chapter – 3	WhatsApp Marketing	31
Chapter – 4	Instagram Marketing	36
Chapter – 5	YouTube Marketing	47
Chapter – 6	Twitter Marketing	53
Chapter – 7	Interactive Marketing	64
Chapter – 8	Mobile Marketing	76
Chapter – 9	Search Engine Marketing (SEM)	87
Chapter – 10	Pay-Per-Click (PPC)	96
Chapter – 11	Social Media Marketing	100
Chapter – 12	Visual Marketing	118
Chapter – 13	Customer Data Platform	125
Chapter – 14	Conclusion	128

References *135*

Chapter – 1

INTRODUCTION TO DIGITAL MARKETING

Introduction

Digital marketing is marketing as well as promotion of goods or services by utilizing digital technologies, especially through the Web, cell phones, visual advertising as well as any other electronic media. Digital marketing platforms are Internet-based and offline systems which can build, promote, and distribute brand quality across digital channels to an end user.

Digital marketing significantly transformed the way companies and corporations employ communication technologies. Digital marketing strategies have become more widespread and effective as online technologies become progressively integrated into business plans as well as daily life, and as consumers utilize digital equipment rather than accessing physical stores.

Digital marketing techniques like search engine marketing (SEM), product management, search engine optimization (SEO), project marketing, information-driven marketing, e-business, social media, electronic-mail marketing, interactive ads, digital books, influencer marketing, spinning disks and gaming have become more popular in today's world. However, digital marketing also applies to offline platforms including digital media, cell phones (SMS or MMS), backup, and smartphone, visual media, etc. Essentially, this expansion of offline platforms helps to distinguish digital marketing towards online marketing.

History

Digital marketing has always been inextricable from technology advancement. One of the key elements is the beginning in 1971, when Ray Tomlinson delivered the first message, and his software established the place for people to transmit and receive data via multiple machines. The more identifiable era is in the beginning of Digital Marketing was 1991, as the Archie browser was developed as an archive of File Transfer Protocol (FTP) pages. Computer memory space had already been high enough to hold huge amounts of customer data. Companies began preferring digital strategies such as advertising servers rather than restricted list brokers. These databases enabled businesses to monitor customer data more efficiently by improving the interaction among buyers and sellers.

The word Digital Marketing had been first introduced in the 1990s. With the advent of server and client computing and the rise of desktop computers, consumer relationship management (CRM) systems had become a major part of communications technology. Fierce competition pushed companies to include more features in their apps, such as advertising, marketing and sales implementations. Marketers have owned large online customer information through E-CRM systems after the Web was created. Organizations should review client needs information and improve their satisfaction. This led to its first searchable banner ad getting listed in 1995, that was the AT&T's "You Can" advertisement and 43 percent of viewers who have seen it have stuck on the commercial during the first few months.

With ever more Online users as well as the launch of iOS in 2001, consumers began to search for goods and to make decisions about their desires digitally first, rather than contacting a salesman, creating a new challenge for a corporate marketing team. However, a study in 2002 showed that all stores hadn't yet declared their individual domains addresses. Such issues made advertisers to seek new ways to develop business.

In 2008, business intelligence idea was introduced to address this above issue. Advertising automation supported consumers in the segment of businesses, introduced multi-channel marketing strategies, and received customer data. Nonetheless, its versatility level for consumer products wasn't good enough.

In 2000 as well as in 2010, online marketing had become more complex, as the explosion of computers capable of receiving digital content contributed to rapid growth. Reports created in 2013 as well as in 2014 indicated development in online marketing. With advancement of technology networks like LinkedIn, Instagram, YouTube and Twitter, customers in everyday life are heavily dependent on digital systems. They wanted a smooth customer experience through multiple channels to find information about the product. Consumer behavior transition increased advertising innovation diversification.

People often recognized the digital marketing, social media marketing, and network marketing is providing value to their life. Online marketing has gained prominence over decades. Internet advertising is still common in many countries. Throughout Europe, online advertising is called Internet marketing. Global online marketing became the most general term, particularly after 2014.

Digital content usage was projected at 4.6 trillion online ads displayed annually with multimedia expenditure, rising 50 percent in 2012. The portion of advertisements comes through online behavioral ads (OBA), companies that target advertisements to online users, however raises concerns around data privacy and confidentiality.

Key Elements of Digital Marketing

Easy access

The main goal of digital marketing is to reach consumers and encourage them to connect with the product via digital technology distribution. Data is easily available by using electronic communications. Users of the Internet may use other digital media like Twitter, YouTube, and Gmail, etc. By Electronic communications, this provides a multi-communication channel whereby data can be easily exchanged by anyone at anywhere in the globe, irrespective of who they really are. Cultural discrimination plays no significant role via social media due to a lack of direct contact or common knowledge to a small community. Its immersive nature requires the customers to build dialogue where specific viewers may pose questions regarding the current product or familiarize themselves with it where the traditional marketing methods may not deliver.

Competitive edge

Businesses may build competitive edge by different means utilizing Web technologies. To meet the highest potential of online marketing, businesses utilize social networks as their key tool to make a stream for data. Through all this, a company will establish a system where consumers can identify patterns of behavior and comment about consumer desires. This medium of advertising has also shown greater impact on someone with a strategic association with both the company and customers who may be general online social media clients. To this effect, developing a good social media account will also improve the satisfying relationship among new buyers and current buyers as well as constant product promotion and thus increasing brand awareness culminating in the Brand recognition Framework for customers. While brand images might be inconsistent; sustaining a positive online presence allows a company to be reliable in communications by establishing a multiple way of information stream. Businesses find their material dependent on data received through such a network, as a consequence of the complex environment created by global nature of technology. Good use of online marketing can contribute comparatively to a low cost compared with traditional marketing methods like reduce external service costing, operating expenses, promotion costs, processing fees, software development costs as well as control costs.

Efficiency

Efficiency of Brand recognition have been shown to work more efficiently in countries which are strong in insecurity resistance, also those places with instability minimization. In such places, online marketing works fantastically. Nonetheless, marketers should be cautious to never be aggressive in using this form of advertising or rely exclusively on it, as it could have consequences which could affect their identity negatively. Brands that anthropomorphize it are much more likely to be successful in cases in which a company is selling to this group. Social networking use might increase product awareness and therefore minimize ambiguity, it really possible that some people with strong confusion and aversion would especially appreciate the higher degree of social media engagement with a humanoid brand. Furthermore, digital platform enables the company and its consumers to communicate directly and share their motivations.

Digital Marketing System

Digital marketing system (DMS) is indeed a hierarchical network management mechanism utilized mainly for goods and services. This incorporates a content management system (CMS) through Internet syndication, desktop and virtual media.

1. Web: A DMS operates web networks, typically as a hold-alone site. This can handle any aspect of the internet system, like website design, hosting services, domain registration, advertising, content development, and other online promoting techniques. Web publishing aims to bring the individual an online environment on the Internet where consumers, visitors, supporters as well as other media players come to a portal. Many digital marketing strategies also operate to route to the website channel.

2. Social media: A DMS uses popular online networks like Facebook and Twitter as a means of communicating to supporters, family, associates, and clients and gain exposure to the websites of the client. The digital publication may come in the form of a Facebook status, a Facebook message, a post, an image, a clip, as well as several other social media. The trick is to find users in social hubs of those who not addressed otherwise. This helps to connect, like social media networks.

3. Mobile: A DMS produces original content for portable devices, such as iPad, iPhone or Android phones. Web publishing is always an online-optimized website style with wider navigation with simpler operating system. A digital publication may also include device-supporting mods, push updates, or SMS message advertising. Gaming is indeed a modern form of online advertising, where developers tailor gaming for only a particular brand. It is the major factor in which the product requires online publishing.

4. Scanner: Platforms for scannable surface contain tablet computer, publication content, TV press, etc. QR code makes traditional advertising platforms for a modern digital transition. A fast QR code scanner will immediately lead audiences to the data they want without spending a lot of time scrolling and checking, as well as the most useful way to use QR code scan would be to connect to purchase goods.

NFC or Close-field networking is an increasing data-sharing tool, i.e. money payments, retrieve information as well as other private information.

Non-Linear Advertising Strategy

To reach consumers, marketers should switch from the static one-way communication marketing strategy to a quality-exchange system of shared interaction and welfare-sharing between the vendor and the buyer. Transactions were more non-linear as well as one-on-one and one and to-many. Knowledge and data could travel through various outlets, like Twittersphere, Twitter, LinkedIn, Instagram, Snapchat, Pinterest, and a number of other networks. Online forums and social media allow people to quickly create material and openly post their views, observations, and feelings and thoughts on several issues and goods, ultra-accelerating the knowledge dissemination.

The Nielsen Global Connected Commerce organized a study and commissioned surveys in 26 nations to see how customers take buying choices in stores and online browsing in the Web. The study indicated that online customers are constantly planning to buy from abroad, with about 50 percent in the study amongst those shopping online over the last six months of the study saying that they ordered from an international store.

Utilizing an omni-channel approach is extremely valuable to businesses that have to adjust to the new demands of customers, who just want increasingly technologically advanced deals across the buying process. Retailers continually concentrate on their Web presence, with online retailers running within traditional shop-based stores. The "unending corridor" inside commercial space could drive customers to buy goods online that solve their problems, because stores don't have to hold the merchandise inside the store's geographic location. Many Web-based merchants often dominate the market. Many create matching shop-based stores that can provide professional services, technical assistance, and meaningful interactions of their goods.

Hence, an omni-channel model helps shoppers, but also helps company bottom line. Research shows that buyers invest more when shopping via an omni-channel store compared to a normal-channel distributor, and are much more attentive. This may be attributed to quick buying and greater product quality.

Types of Data

Basic information: Traditionally, personal information primarily involves race, sex, history, employment status and much other general information. Personal information often involves specific digital data, like passwords, in Web culture. Unlawful use of data. The debate about the implications of privacy concerns raised by online marketing technologies was primarily centered on the risk of inappropriately accessing data. Business information can become products and it can be sold or transferred without consumer choice or approval.

Consumer data: It is primarily shared and transacted in several ways. The first is that the relevant retailers exchange this information. Another is that some may offer these information to a third party. For instance, information that can define customer financial situation is quite valuable to credit reporting agencies. These raise online privacy risk.

Consumer disposition: Many consumers tend to choose between confidentiality as well as other ideal circumstances. Evidence indicates that some consumers are prepared to allow retailers to use private information like they have something to benefit in exchange, even when they do care regarding their confidentiality. Furthermore, online marketing offers people comfort. Many consumers find this comfort more valuable than their safety, particularly for teenagers. Nonetheless, many people are worried with preserving their confidentiality.

Supervision and administration: Advertising authorization seems like a great way to address regulatory and privacy concerns. This offers a convenient way of connecting retailers with consumers. Customers can only permit a certain vendor, selected from a significant number of traders. Authorization marketing focuses on making digital advertising suit the demand of the law and provide data independence for customers. Other approach is to publish data reports to encourage openness and transparency.

The Global Data Protection Regulation (GDPR) exemplifies the latter criteria. This stipulates that retailers can only gather customer data for relevant, valid and lawful reasons and comply with in a reasonable, open and reasonable manner, and marketers should safeguard those data. Consumers should be told that this is how their data would be used, what would be the consequences and other related information in a descriptive, simple-to-understand and standardized so that they would easily decide if approval is needed or not. Besides the obligation to be updated, the GDPR gives consumers several other freedoms, such as the right to access, the right to deletion, the right to limit storage, the right to complain, and the related transparency mechanism.

Modern Strategies

Some of the key changes to traditional marketing are related to the emergence of digital marketing, which contributed to the reinvention of marketing strategies to respond to this major change in traditional marketing. Because digital marketing relies on ever-evolving and fast-changing technologies, the same innovations should be anticipated from digital media.

Collaboration atmosphere: A collaboration framework can be formed between the company, the software supplier, and online agencies to maximize initiative, sharing of resources, availability, and interactions. In fact, companies encourage their clients to better understand and to represent them. This data source is named "user-generated data". Much will be learned by various websites in which the agency allows people to discuss suggestions which are then tested by other users on the site. The most common concepts were analyzed and somehow applied. Using such an approach of collecting information and creating new goods will promote organizations interaction with their clients as well as breeding innovations which is often ignored.

Data-driven advertising: Consumers produce a lot of information in each and every move they make on the consumer experience route, and

Brands can still use the information to enable their established audience through data-driven purchasing. By compromising the identity of consumers, user information can be obtained through digital channels. For example, if users purchase a product, receive an e-mail, or release, or connect with the mobile app of the brand, marketers may also collect data through real-world social interactions, such as trips to stores, or CRM and marketing algorithm databases. Often recognized as Individuals-based Marketing and Addressable Content, Data-driven advertisement empowers advertisers to identify their potential customers in their marketplace and provide far more personal contact, extremely relevant to the time and behavior of each consumer. When settling on a plan today, an important factor is that online tools globalized the marketing environment.

Remarketing: Remarketing is critical in online marketing. This strategy helps advertisers to post targeted advertisements before an interest group or a given demographic, typically called Internet searchers, either looking for particular goods or services or visiting a website for a certain reason.

Gameplay advertisement: Gaming advertisements are video and computer games promotion. Among the most notable examples in-game advertising are sporting billboard. In-game advertisements may also occur as brand names like weapons, vehicles, and clothes that serve as game status symbols.

The modern digital age has allowed marketers to approach their buyers individually, possibly involved to their product, based on past surfing preferences. Companies can use social networks to pick the age group, place, sex and preferences they want to see from their targeted message. However, regarding the recent browsing history of a consumer, they can also be followed on the Web to see ads with different companies, services and products, allowing businesses to reach the same consumers they know and understand. It will most profit through their good or service, something which has limited capacity till the Internet age.

Trying to balance searching and displaying: Balancing searching and displaying for display screen advertising is important. Advertisers usually look at the last quest and assign all the output. This then lacks other marketing campaigns that assess brand equity within the mind of the customers. Com Score calculated by analyzing information online which was generated by about one hundred multi-channel marketers that digital display advertising offered more advantages as opposed to paid advertising. So, it is recommended that when somebody tries to click a display advertisement the client should activate a webpage and not just the homepage. Frequently advertisers see higher sales from a search ad which is exposed to individuals. Yet remember how often users can touch with a show program relative to a quest project. Multichannel marketers have expanded scope by using the show in conjunction to search initiatives. Generally, all quest and advertising elements are respected as show strategies create brand recognition. So, more people are likely to view on digital ads while conducting a searching campaign.

Knowing Mobile: Understanding phones and tablets is also an important aspect of online marketing since phones and tablets already contribute for a significant percent of the time for the online users. Phones provide both a great opportunity and an obstacle to advertisers, as first of all the software requires to be installed and furthermore, the person wants to be used. This can be daunting because half of the time expended on smartphone apps happens on the sole most-used device and nearly 85 percent of their usage on the highest four classified devices. Mobile ads may help achieve a range of business goals and is successful when controlling the entire display, so speech and reputation is likely to be extremely regarded; although the advertisement should not be seen or deemed invasive. Digital media drawbacks on portable devices have included reduced artistic skills and scope. Even though there have been several positive elements, including consumers right to access product details, digital media provides a versatile messaging forum and direct selling opportunity.

Cross-platform assessment: Advertising platforms continue to grow which increase scope. Use a cross-platform approach to unify consumer assessment and press strategy. Marketing experts need to consider how the omni-channel impacts the consumer habits, though that is not assessed while ads are on consumer products. Significant facets of cross-platform calculation include de-duplication and recognition that you will have achieved a cumulative point with another channel, rather than more experiences of already met users. An instance was ESPN with com score on Operation Blueprint, finding that the sports journalist generated a 21 percent growth in uncomplicated average coverage by online advertising. TV and radio are mass networks, dealing with online and other new ads. Nevertheless, TV ads does not directly compete with modern online advertising because it can cross channels through computer technology. Radio also takes power by cross-platform sharing media. TV and radio tend to convince and impact listeners through different platforms.

Targeting, display capacity, product security and invalid traffic: Targeting, viewability, brand protection and unconstitutional traffic have all been features used by advertisers to promote online advertising. Cookies are really a form of online advertisement which tracks resources inside mobile devices. It may cause difficulties, include removal by internet browsers, inability to arrange devices among different users, unreliable figures for unique users, disproportionate scope, intensity comprehension, ad server issues that could not be differentiated between when the cookies are removed.

Platforms for Digital Marketing

Online advertising is enabled by various channels in digital marketing. As an advertising company one's core goal is to seek avenues that are contributing to greater two-way communication with significantly better return for the product. There may be several digital advertising services available.

*1. **Affiliate Marketing**:* Affiliate Marketing is regarded as the simple method for Internet marketing. This may be indicative of a lack of quality with related to affiliates to deliver the required range of new clients. As a consequence of this threat, this makes the company vulnerable to manipulation in terms of alleging commission which is not genuinely acquired. Legal avenues can offer protection against all of this; however, there are limits to retrieving any setback or income. Nonetheless, affiliate advertising helps the company to appeal for smaller publishers or high-traffic sites. Brand names that want to use this strategy must also be warned of such threats and must aim to collaborate with partners with whom protocols are defined between both the parties concerned to maintain or reduce the risk associated.

*2. **Display ads**:* As the word indicate, digital advertising concerns with showing virtual marketing advertisements and information for users. It covers a wide variety of ads such as ad forums, platforms, audio ads, semantic information, Web browser ads, categorized and interactive ads, etc. The approach may focus on specific viewers tuned in to watch a single commercial, the differences can be seen as one of the most efficient aspect of this process.

*3. **Email marketing**:* Compared to other types of online marketing, electronic mail advertising is actually cheap. However, it is a method of communication to a notification such as its business model to current or prospective customers. Nevertheless, receivers can view such communication channel as irritating and annoying particularly to fresh or prospective customers, so that the effectiveness of email ads depends on the vocabulary and aesthetic appeal of the content implemented and therefore it is important. With regard to visual appeal, there have been suggestions that the use of graphic and sound effects to the document is important can be sent, but use of less visual images to original email messages are seen to be more successful for providing a more private email experience. The design is the key factor in deciding how mesmerizing the email is. Using relaxed voice evokes a cooler and friendly email sound relative to a formal environment. For configurations, it is recommended to increase efficiency; without using any graphics or visual that accompanying informal speech. Also, by contrast, to use no aesthetic appeal and simple language may be less effective.

4. *Search Engine Marketing:* Search Engine Marketing (SEM) is an Internet marketing strategy that entails supporting websites by enhancing their exposure on search engine resources pages (SERPs) mainly via paid advertisements. SEM may implement Search Engine Optimization that updates or revise Web content structure to improve pay per click (PPC) rankings in search engine outcome platforms.

5. *Social Web Marketing:* The word "Digital Marketing" seems to have a variety of advertising aspects, as it embraces multiple channels used during as well as among them arrives social media. Using social media platforms (Facebook, Twitter, Pinterest, Snapchat, Google$^+$, etc.) to advertise a service or product has always been named as social media advertising. This is a process where tactics are created and implemented to generate attention for a Webpage or to capture Internet buyers' interest through various social media channels.

6. *Social networking site:* Social networking is indeed an online service used by users to build the necessary networks as well as social relationships with others who share a common personal or professional preferences, hobbies, experiences and actual-life contacts.

7. *In-game advertising:* In-game promotion is characterized as using brands or products in such a digital game. The game allows companies or companies to sell ads in their match, in either a subtle way or in the shape of an advertisements banner. There are several factors as to whether marketers are effective in advertisement of their product or brand, such as: game type, technology, etc.

Evaluation the Efficiency of Digital Marketing Processes

The greatest requirements for evaluating any company must be its rate of return or other economic metrics. In particular, the requirements and methodologies for evaluating digital advertising campaigns could be discussed in more detail.

Requirements and indicators can be categorized by form and time period. They can either test such initiatives quantitatively or qualitatively. Quantifiable metrics can include volume of sales and profits increase or decrease. Whereas, qualitative indicators can be included improved "brand recognition, logo, image and well-being" and "client relationship".

Diverting attention to the period, they may need to calculate several "Long term Metrics," which provides some perspective during a journey as a whole, as well as to assess some "Final Indicators" at the end of the journey to remind the user whether the overall effort has been effective or not. For instance, some social media measures and measurements such as clicks, views, and audience responses can be categorized as intermediate indicators while the current sales amount increase or decrease is obviously from the final classification. All types should be associated. However, a poor result could end the digital marketing procedure and is given in the expectation of earlier perceived progress during the venture.

Digital marketing strategy is a brand development concept. This defines the first phase of digital marketing planning for both the wider digital advertising process. The distinction between modern and conventional campaign strategy is that it uses the electronic communication tools and techniques such as Facebook, Internet, Phone, and Scannable Screen. Moreover, these must fit with the firm's dream, purpose, and overall corporate strategy.

Digital Marketing Planning Stages

Following Dr. Dave Chaffey's methodology, digital marketing management (DMP) includes three main phases: opportunity, strategy and action. He says that any company pursuing an effective digital marketing campaign should organize the project by focusing on the possibilities, objectives and behavior. This conventional strategic approach always has stages of scenario analysis, establishing targets, formulating plans, allocating resources, and tracking.

1. **Opportunity:** To make an efficient DMP, a company must first study the global market and has to set targets like specific, quantifiable, workable, appropriate as well as time bound. Through evaluating the current business metrics and main performance measures the company must develop these targets. It is important to tailor the metrics used in the performance measure the firm formulate, priorities, purpose and dream. Organizations may search sales and marketing gaps by evaluating their existing distribution and impact dissemination. It ensures that they have such a competitive edge as their co-marketers' power and brand relations can be evaluated.

To suddenly stop the chance, the company must sum up the persons of its existing customers and conclude their digital advertising ability from such a purchase path. This implies that they have to have a clear understanding of who they are presently and also how many assets they may assign to their online marketing strategy. Through summing up the buying process, we may also identify holes or potential for possible business opportunities that neither meet goals and suggest new goals or boost profits.

2. **Strategy:** To generate a scheduled social media strategy, the business must review its digital proposal (what you deliver to customers) and interact it using digital consumer-centric methods. We must therefore describe the Online Quality Proposal, implying the business should explicitly articulate what it offers by online to consumers, e.g.: brand placement.

The organization should also select target audience groups and individuals and identify virtual advertising strategies. Thereafter, it is necessary to update the promotional strategy of online options. Marketing mix includes the 4Ps: Product, Price, Place, and Promotion. Few researchers introduced three new factors to the conventional marketing, like process, place and physical appearance and 4Ps, bringing it as the 7Ps of marketing.

3. *Implementation:* The final step involves the company to set up plan and network topologies, which must be tangible to touch points, like viewers throughout all platforms. Therefore, advertisers should ensure that the plan and management tools combine the company's compensated controlled and received news. The Implementation or final preparation phase often allows the company for to develop tangible material, e.g.: audio, graphical and published digital media. In order to approve the online marketing strategy, a planned electronic communications template should be stored across the company's activities. It means that all channels used remain in formation and support one another for successive digital marketing campaign levels.

4. *Customer awareness:* Another way in which advertisers can meet customers and recognize their thinking process is based on what is considered as an awareness graph. There is a four-step chart for understanding. The first move is to ask any questions which the customer feels in their statistics. The second option is to explain the customer's feelings. Third is to talk on what the user will suggest in the case. The last step is to visualize whatever the customer wants to do depending on other three stages. This map allows marketing departments to position oneself in their consumer boots. Web data analysis is also an essential way of understanding customers. It tells about the Internet habits of people in each site. A specific form of such analysis is quantitative analytics that helps advertisers to decide in which road customers are still on. It gathers information obtained from many other researches and creates different forecasts about what the customers are doing and then, to allow businesses to formulate a strategy about what has to be done next, as per the patterns in the communities.

5. *Sharing economy:* The "sharing economy" relates to a financial pattern aimed at obtaining an unused resource. The sharing economy has had an unprecedented impact on several elements, like jobs, manufacturing, and distribution network. It is not insignificant that some sectors are clearly under pressure. Sharing economy affects traditional advertising strategies by changing the structure of a particular concept involving possession, resources, and hiring.

Digital marketing platforms and traditional advertising networks are identical that a supply chain moves quality product and service from the original seller to the end consumer. For example, a traditional virtual medium is email. Company can monitor the user's operation and advertisement details by sending and receiving newsletter or e-mail. Besides this standard approach, the designed-in power, flexibility and low price of digital marketing platforms are basic features in shared economy implementation.

Conclusion

Clients often search the Internet, then purchase in shops, scan in retail outlets, and then look for other affordable options. Online brand consumer analysis is especially popular for greater-priced items and consumer products like food and cosmetics. Customers frequently use the Web to check information about the product, check prices, and look for sales and offers.

There are many ways to companies to use online marketing to support their marketing campaigns. The use online marketing in an Internet age not only enables companies to sell their products and services, but it also facilitates virtual customer service across 24/7 services that make clients feel comfortable and respected. Social networking engagement helps marketers to gain response both positively and negatively from the consumers to decide which media networks fit well enough for them. Online marketing is becoming a growing asset to companies and enterprises. Customers use social networking outlets, forums, or sites to share reviews about their interaction with a specific product digitally. Using these interactions via their social networks is becoming incredibly popular for companies to have personal contact with the public and handle the input they obtain accordingly.

Social media or peer-to-peer networking often get a greater impact on consumers because they are not delivered directly from the manufacturer and thus not anticipated. Consumers are much more inclined to trust other clients' views. It was observed in an Instagram experiment where scientists found that teen Facebook users posted photos of food related interactions inside their social media, offering free ads for goods.

Organizations are constantly utilizing social media sites to communicate to their clients and build such conversations and discussions. Social media growth was demonstrated by reality that the Facebook app had much more than 127 million active average visitors per month in 2016, and YouTube had over 98 million daily active viewers.

Chapter - 2

FACEBOOK MARKETING

Introduction

During the first years of social media networking, the biggest player was MySpace. Around 2004 and 2007, it expanded to 100 million people, and by 2008, people visited this site much more than Google. Then Facebook arrived. According to a report from "Our History" in *Facebook,* Facebook exceeded MySpace in global usage in 2009. Facebook advertising relates to developing a Facebook page as just a channel of communication to keep in touch with others and attract more customers. Facebook openly offers for this and enabling users to share individual statuses or page for businesses, groups, and any other organization working on developing an audience for a brand, product, or service.

It is very minimum and it is important to have a business Web page for companies and it is much simpler to develop. If you have a premium brand or a small company with only a couple of people, you can guarantee that certain clients are on Facebook. Generally, companies use Facebook ads for food, appliances, household goods, eateries, etc. practically any product can be marketed via Facebook, transforming casual consumers into enthusiastic fans following news of sales and innovations and connecting to their own mates.

Local business: How well a shop is family-owned or perhaps a bigger firm's franchise, a Facebook page could be used to transform a regional client base in to a supporter base visiting the stores more frequently.

Personalities, singers, actors, writers, syndicated journalists and anyone who earns money by being listed on Facebook like to be remembered for much more people as possible. On-profit companies, charitable organizations, organizations, and public service programs can all exploit Facebook's existing networking capability.

Although originally invented for university students, Facebook has grown much further than that. According to "Facebook.com Traffic, Demographics and Competitors – Alexa," nearly a quarter of all consumers are in the 18–34 age group and significantly more than a quarter of users are female. Around half of the profiles were reached by portable devices or laptops. Due to its high number of users, there is indeed a wide range of product categories which can be attained on Facebook and an international fan platform for almost any growing market.

There are more useful Facebook product queries like, when is the Facebook advertising most efficient? etc. If brand or business websites are more effective, daily articles that are posted in the morning draw more attention than evening reports. Usually, customers who use the platform from home can look at Facebook at any point throughout the day. Working and college-going users check Facebook pre and post work/school. Thus, just sharing during most of the business day lacks most openings.

Facebook pages are sometimes connected to company Web pages elsewhere in the Web. So, sometimes, it is a great idea to use all of the same details in both locations to retain continuity. A company website can be checked for as long as it is online, and unlike a personal page, you can't invite people by this. Business pages don't get "family," "fans"— and then, that contrast makes the difference. To build an original seed base for both the fans, every marketing department member must begin by enjoying the business page of their own Facebook profiles and all workers must be invited to join. When a person likes a site, Facebook automatically adds this occurrence to their profile and each of their buddies can see this action.

Different Applications of Facebook

- Organize the Facebook blog page and your Facebook page
- Send people a sign-up to your updates through your Page on Facebook
- Request consumer feedback
- Encourage social networking interaction, like Facebook
- Create promotional materials and other material which can be published via Facebook
- Organize Internet marketing initiatives, like Facebook, Twitter, industry forums, sites, and affiliate services
- Establish advertising targets and indicators via Facebook and measure performance
- Develop promotional campaigns for brands and
- Allocate and track groups to produce content on Facebook page Products
- Link the Channel on YouTube to Facebook
- Manage unique marketing tasks, like managing Facebook fans virtual competition
- Add sweepstakes to the face book page site
- Promote internal and external, such that staff of an organization are much more likely to join the firm's Facebook supporter base

Education and Experience

All Facebook users who follows a site may see some material that a company updates and also be informed of comments from their social media feeds. When that material activates them, they will report in it, and like the product. In fact, they can upload this material that will add the full content with their own pages, and remind their mates to try looking up. Therefore, the firm's job is to facilitate this procedure.

Interaction and stability are the most vital aspect of Facebook product marketing. Generating a Page on Facebook, and afterwards abandoning this alone, may not net anything on an enterprise. In order to attract viewers, a company have to frequently post fresh content in various formats so other users can see and re-Tweet the site. Material can advertise new deals, highlight particular products or individuals, exchange interesting facts, include promotional keys for services and products offers, and everything that captures fans' attention.

As Facebook's news content works, a comment's perceived strength is a key factor in coordinating how much a user understands. An average consumer has over 130 contacts, and could even be a fan of many products, celebrities, and institutions. While signing up, there is no way to immediately display action from either of these outlets.

Facebook feed displays updates from colleagues. They communicate with almost all, and they are similar and lighter. However, a firm's article is expected to be only available on social media feeds for around three times from the time they publish it. However, based on the time during the day when they write, totally different parts of the supporter base are expected to view it.

Besides varied material and layout, posts will allow consumers to connect and react. Companies can provide clear calls for action, which could be as easy as "look at this," "like the above," or "express this." Alternatively, companies can promote engagement by competitions and surveys, that are the ways to gather market research. These small-commitment efforts foster interaction and customer-based connection.

Many marketing executives has at least a basic understanding, often in promotion, branding, or marketing, and significant popular online trading expertise. They ought to be social networks or internet business systems specialists. Training them for such a profession covers advertising courses, research and analysis, market trends, and focus on online retail activity.

Many brand directors had at least a shred in marketing or advertising, and extensive positive practice in designing and managing marketing strategies. We should learn how to promote on various channels, like social networks. Training for this field requires courses in graphic arts, competitive analysis, and consumer preferences.

Media relations executives must have a graduate degree, typically in public affairs or communication systems; approximately one-fourth should have masters in related subject. Executives seem to have a degree in promotion company management and marketing. Employees need an experience throughout all channels of communication, particularly social networks. Professional experience also starts with an apprentice helping more skilled employees, and reporting for a business newsletters or website. Such abilities include outstanding communication and research skills, organization and leadership.

Few Considerations of the Facebook Business Page

- *Provide product and company information:* If you are not proving the specifics of your company or brand, nobody can approach your business.

- *Attractiveness:* It is important to have an attracting cover picture apart from a good profile image.

- *Consistency:* Maintains the consistency of the brand' and elegance is important for a good Facebook page.

- *Updating the page:* Update the page with entry and insightful material.

- *Facebook favorite:* Frequently attach your favorite on your Facebook page.

- *Organize the page:* Appointment of experts to run the site efficiently is good otherwise page may go down or be hacked.

- *Emotional picture:* Emotive symbolism is a good way to get the attention of people.

- *Continuity:* Continuity is essential in upgrading for style and works of the page.

- *Quality:* Eliminates hundreds of boring and dreary comments each week and focus on quality material.

- *Stay positive:* Use the tone which making your site a place where people feel better.

- *Enjoyment:* An amusing appearance would establish a more appealing image to the page.

- *Balance:* An effective site requires creating a content and business led post equilibrium. Include fun, instructional, and interesting content to promote engagement.

Conclusion

Successful Facebook advertising requires an ability to utilize social networks efficiently, encouraging users to maximize their engagement. A brilliant marketing program helps to improve both customer awareness and strong communication abilities. Advertising should show them how and when to better explain your customers. Market research courses (including statistical analysis) can help you identify and reach different market segments. You will have to learn how to recognize and adapt to shifts in supply and demand, and how to manage different market trends and opportunities. As online business and social media rapidly changing the sector, specific study courses should train you for these environments and help you understand why consumers function differently in this context than in the traditional market setting.

A further key focus in a marketing plan is messaging. Consumers are not only to know where to interact via a number of different ways and platforms at an advertising school, but you will also need to develop talking and interpersonal skills into your other courses. People may study often marketing contact and corporate and digital communication. Similarly, you will connect not only by letters, but by images, photos, maps, as well as other media. This capability range will also be critical while using social networks to support the clients, as you are using various methods to target various product categories.

Chapter - 3

WHATSAPP MARKETING

Introduction

Whenever we talk about social networks, sites like YouTube, Facebook and Twitter immediately come to our mind. Also, chat applications have probably caught user-friendly social networking. Advertising is gradually utilizing messaging software. The globe's pioneer is WhatsApp with 1,6 billion registered as monthly users worldwide.

This consumer growth cannot be overlooked. The question is: How can you successfully sell in WhatsApp? As with all largely unexplored frontlines, early investors face similar risks and rewards. Here are some WhatsApp's marketing references.

WhatsApp

WhatsApp is indeed a free downloadable application that allows your phone's Internet service to permit you to communicate to many WhatsApp customers without paying. You can also exchange documents and photos, and promote free video conferencing and calls.

Supporting a wide variety of devices also made it incredibly common in areas with large SMS costs. This is the most convenient alternative for SMS for nations and people in general.

Although Facebook purchased WhatsApp and since then it has served as a distinct entity and has not shown the same advertising-friendly functionality in Facebook Messenger.

WhatsApp provides iOS, Mac, Windows and Nokia S40 models. There is a Web interface and online apps for Mac or Windows Computers, but you are required to downloaded it on your cell phone, because each WhatsApp profile is linked directly to just one. When a consumer installs the software, you have to check your nation or input your cell number. You could either upload your Facebook data with one tap or physically insert a photo and attach a username which you can modify later.

WhatsApp utilizes mobile numbers in your list of contacts to give you an update that your WhatsApp app file you already know Someone with your mobile number in their phone contacts list will also immediately see your page if you adjust your privacy controls.

Like many messaging services, you could talk with the other client into your phone's contacts. We may also call and send voice samples with them.

Group chats let you exchange comments, images, and videos with up to 256 people at once. Everybody in the group chat will put a word in the chat to see the answers of everybody else.

If you deliver a message to the list, it can go to anybody in the contact who saves your number in the contacts list of their mobiles. We will see the response as a regular post, equivalent to the BCC feature of text. When they answer, it will show into your chats monitor as a standard one-to one email. So, their response cannot be sent to anybody in the transmitted folder.

Importance of WhatsApp for Business

The strongest reason in engaging WhatsApp is that several of the clients are also likely to using it. Each day, WhatsApp sends more over 60 billion notifications.

Remarkably, WhatsApp consumers and online services are able to do marketing. As per Facebook Messaging Report, over the next couple years, 69 percent of social messaging service consumers say that they plan to use more talk to connect to companies. However, 53 percent of those surveyed claim they are most willing to shop with such a company they can specifically share their communications.

For your clients and stakeholders are youthful, often they are very prone to be confident using messaging services for regular communication. A study by Pew Research Center revealed that 43 percent of mobile phone users aged 18-29 utilized messaging services including WhatsApp, relative to just 19 percent of mobile phone users aged 50 and over.

In fact, messaging services like WhatsApp has impressive activation rates. 98 percent of smartphone notifications are accessed and interpreted, with 90percent opening within three seconds of receiving them.

WhatsApp Marketing Strategies and Tips

WhatsApp does not really offer advertising space and have any marketing specific facility so the marketing approach must be creative to use of your marketing activity.

Although WhatsApp is unique in its scope and functionality than other chat applications. designing your WhatsApp strategies parallel to your broader communication marketing plan is essential.

Still there are some drawbacks to tackle when designing the WhatsApp marketing plan. There is really no business account, hence if the product establishes a login it has the same constraints like any other client.

As each WhatsApp profile is directly linked to a specific mobile number and you can only post at WhatsApp accounts at once, it is not a good choice for big, one-to-many advertising. Therefore, the chances of success are better if you take full advantage of its drawbacks.

Like other instant messaging facilities, portion of WhatsApp's strength is that it is tied to our devices, which seem more private to us than our computer systems, yet they are not expressed and we carry them all over. The advertising campaigns you discuss should represent and regard its personal element. Consumers connect with their colleagues, so confidence and imagination are important.

WhatsApp Marketing Tools

WhatsApp introduced a Commercial App that they claim that "made with a the minor business person in mind". The service is free to access, and currently only accessible for Android. It allows companies to communicate readily with clients using techniques to optimize, form, and rapidly reply to communications.

For instance, you can go in and recycling frequently and sent texts using these "quick answers" to better reply common issues. Consumers can also place a text away if you cannot reply instantly, so your clients know when and how to anticipate a response. There is also a salutation message that greets clients for your business. Install a free book to enhance social networking interaction with better viewer research, clearer consumer targeting, and simple-to-use social networking software.

Since WhatsApp offers no business techniques or an Application Programming Interface (API), aimed small-scale initiatives like the explanations are the best approach. To begin to talk to people, contribute your number to a contacts list of your mobile. WhatsApp offers a way to attach a swipe-to-chat connection to your homepage, mail signature, and social media accounts, making it possible for people to begin a product discussion.

Bear in mind that perhaps the assumption in communication is for close-instant responses, so ensure you have had the resources to handle the chats and limit accessibility to particular time window bars.

WhatsApp third-party marketing schemes and services available to add multiple WhatsApp transactions and marketing expert groups, by using them may result with you being partially blocked or totally banned from provider. Moreover, mass communication in this type of setting can endanger your product a lot.

Conclusion

WhatsApp might still be a major way that your community to create content via deep social and a word to explain how people are sharing information through unofficial channels including email. In reality, a vast majority of successful sharing now exists on unofficial channels such as messaging services. Even if you do not use WhatsApp to sell your brand, your potential is probably to use it to spread awareness about your material.

Although WhatsApp is not as marketing-rich as Facebook, it is heading in the right direction. Marketers who build ads with - not just against - WhatsApp's unique features will also have benefit. The scarcity of ads or institutional influence on WhatsApp means regular adopters really can stick out - if wrong.

Social media travels quickly and keeping pace with change - new technologies and changing methodologies - can also be difficult. Know the basic digital marketing abilities you have to keep ahead with free lessons.

Chapter – 4

INSTAGRAM MARKETING

Introduction

Instagram has been one of the quickest growing social media platforms. In 2018, the user base increased to 1 billion. Statistics show how Instagram have a significant impact on people and companies and working on a regular basis. It is a primary source of amusement, education, networking, and business. There is a major barrier for companies to get on the Instagram advertising movement. Many are reflecting by themselves that from where they really begin. It may be disheartening to sift through all disorganized suggestions and tools.

Instagram Marketing Definition and Tactics

Instagram advertising is a form of social media marketing where advertisers utilize Instagram platform to promote their companies. Instagram advertising can entail a variety of different tools and techniques used to meet all sorts of targets a company ought to have. Paid strategies such as online advertising innovator and unpaid techniques such as generating organic content like Tweets, Facebook stories and reviews are really interacting with many other users' content. Traditional business targets may include promoting the goods or services, having more fans participating, build relationships with customers as well as other brands, and basically improving their own brand.

Examples of Instagram Marketing

1. Organic content: Organic content is indeed a term to explain any unregulated material you publish, such as images, clips, or articles. Such videos should be in the core of your Instagram marketing plan, so you can hold your followers naturally and can transform the purchases much simpler.

2. Instagram Advertising: If you are hoping for unbreakable revenue, Instagram ads are a much more logical approach to advertising than inbound links. You may run many types of ads, such as picture ads, video advertising, carnival ads, narrative ads, and shoppable posts.

3. Photo and Video advertising: These ads come up in app notifications the very same way in which articles does in other users and the advertising can also be in the front or center of the customer experience. As you might have expected, a photo ad applies to an ad which shows a picture, and a banner ad contains a video. Such advertisements provide a "send to action button" which prompts customers to take particular action, such as Instagram stories. As per the results, the marketers' portion of ad spending on Stories ads increased every year from ten percent to 19 percent. It may offer good customer satisfaction. These also have a small "Sponsored" key on the upper right and a deem-to-action on the bottommost.

To earn money from Story advertisements, conduct a campaign that highlights your product or service and make sure you attach a request to an action at the bottom to allow consumers to buy.

Instagram Shopping

In 2018, Instagram launched a good feature which allow consumers to buy products without unlocking the app. It is known as Instagram Shopping. The key capability of the latest feature allows companies to label goods in the Instagram posts, during which the potential buyers who select marked objects will also be taken directly to the product page of firm's website.

Let us imagine you are a manufacturer of women's clothing, and there are photos of a model wearing some of your stuff. Prospective customers may click and purchase the product from the mobile device.

As Instagram Marketing is accepted as a vendor, you can sell goods through post and reports. There is even an opportunity to build an Instagram storefront if you are taking up things. For this, you are required to have a Facebook business profile page to use this feature.

If you are really unfamiliar with all of this, you should review Instagram Shopping's comprehensive guide. It is really a serious investigation of how the functionality works and how you can incorporate into the Instagram business plan, and how can boost your picture-sharing app accessibility.

Influencer Marketing

Influencer marketing is now one of contemporary and most popular Internet advertising forms. Instagram influencers are individuals who have evolved natural, committed to their product market in every sector, from apparel to software to banking. Yet influencers generally exist on almost all social networking sites you know about. Whether you find the right influencers to suit the product, this can offer you a massive boost in fans, revenue, and brand awareness. There, the key is finding the correct influencers.

How to Create an Instagram Business Profile

You need to have two things to create an Instagram company profile. An Instagram account that could be your current individual profile or a fresh one that you have built for business. Creating a new address can be considered for your corporate identity that can be used for image building.

You need to create a profile for your corporate Facebook page, for identification purposes, and to use Instagram. Here's a stage by stage glossary to creating your Instagram business account.

- Sign in with your client username on your mobile.

- Click the bottom on the right-side circular symbol. The monitor opens to reveal another list. Tap "Settings" at right side on bottom.

- To create the Instagram profile, move down and find "Move to Business Profile" onto the Settings screen. Change to Instagram Business Page. Instagram would then allow you to link to your Facebook Personal page and update your Business Social Contact details: email, contact number as well as place. It will be available on your page, so you can stop adding personal information.

Create a Good Instagram Business Profile

When optimizing the Instagram page, preparation to stay consistent to the brand is essential. It implies even with the same shades, layouts and pictures you have in another place, of your site as well and other social media profiles. It allows you to facilitate your company clearly and recognizably. The account includes two key elements: the image and the bio data. We consider using your own corporate logo for the image. This assists to improve brand identity, so most businesses are using this approach.

Some Tips to Render Guaranty to Gets Some Publicity

Create it keeping the consumers in mind, not just for your own company. Explain the benefits and significance that you are providing. Use it as an opportunity to advance some major events and material on sale. Instagram hacks allow users to participate to your brand to modify your Instagram page. Your bio will bring consumers to encounter your product, whether it is through a reference to your site or through a direct selling or social bookmarking sites tools.

Instagram Features for Businesses

- ***Instagram Business Features***

Instagram has several useful features to bind people and enhance connections. Even though you are not a regular Instagram user, you probably already know about the most famous features like videos feature, live videos, stories feature, etc.

- ***Hashtags Instagram***

Nowadays, it looks like hashtags are practically all over the Web. When added for your marketing plan, Instagram hashtags are really a clear indication of fans for your photos and are important to whatever information they are searching for. Indeed, several users seek information based on hashtags alone. And, if your comments are linked to the trending subject, please included the corresponding tag. It can assist you to go in front of people who are generally concerned about what to say. You can check the Instagram search function to identify common hashtags or context material shared by others.

- ***Effectiveness of Instagram hashtag***

Other interesting applications include Keyword Designer which build hashtags based on keywords. Most of these techniques offers free outcomes, but necessitate a remunerated upgrade for larger profiles. This is also an intelligent idea to build and use a labeled hashtag regularly. This hashtag may include title of your corporation or a particular campaign, incident, or advertising name.

Over the years millions of users utilizing Instagram stories. Sensibility makes more emotional aspect. They are much fun or transient way to communicate with your fans, as they will only be 10 seconds long, they vanish after 12 hours, and they are not highlighted in your main page or timeline. Stories can be wonderful attraction for your Instagram marketing plan, because they offer you the ability to focus about issues that are more topical or in-depth.

- *Instagram Live*

As the title implies, Instagram Live is a program that allows one to reach the followers in a live stream environment. It is a useful tool particularly when you host an event and address something important or immediate.

The straight mechanism regarding Instagram Live seems to be that your post should present first in the stream of your fans, and they will also get confirmation that it is occurring once they touch the screen. However, with more power comes more obligations. You should use this tool if you have some quality content to post otherwise it may drive away the customers from the page.

- *Marketing strategy for Instagram*

Like every other approach, Instagram advertising strategy will work best when you have a clear objective. Select persons and tactics which will slowly you build and move toward the aim, and keep the track in your advancement all along in such a manner that you can modify wherever necessary.

1. *Objectives:* The targets are foundations in your marketing strategy. We like the Intelligent terminology for goal setting:

2. *Precise:* Give exact figures or targets rather than a fuzzy target.

3. *Measurable:* Select objectives that are traceable and quantifiable with data analysis and perspectives.

4. *Accessible:* Be logical. Probably, a million subscribers per week would not happen.

5. *Relevant:* Stay connected to your market, sector, and perspective.

6. *Time-bound:* Offer yourselves a timeline for your target.

So rather than thinking, "I would like more fans," consider something such as, "My aim is to win 500 real supporters in six months." Instead,

"I need more revenues," seek, "My aim is to receive Rs.1,00000 in profit from Instagram Advertising purchases every month," etc.

Instagram Content Strategy

As mentioned previously, we have several uploading choices to develop the Instagram digital content strategy. Selecting the right versions requires knowing the target. The person has to ask himself about the demography of audience and interest, what they like to do and experience. Who inspires or excites them? How should marketers build confidence and inspire them to buy?

The company may certainly not immediately learn all these responses that are completely normal. It is a great learning experience to have an understanding of Instagram content strategy. However, when you get a sensor-focused view of your target as well as which aspects make them unique, your marketing plan would get stronger and stronger.

Instagram Marketing Strategy

Gain useful insight from the friends as well as rivals.

When you are just heading out, seeing what other businesses are referring to it could be a great help to grow. Find out highest-performing content from related companies, the main rivals, industry champions, and programs which have top successful accounts. Doing the whole strategic study will scoop you off to bring towards the next level critical patterns, good practices, and the little-known techniques. Try to build a timeline of Web content and keep a track. Develop a social online content schedule so that you can really keep on top in your Instagram digital strategy, ensuring it is organized and reliable. Plan out the content for the next period. Plan a minimum of three updates per week. When you are looking for ideas or have trouble selling in all spaces, using free models that mimic popular topic, types and famous comments from other companies.

Few Strategies to Expand Instagram

1. Host a Promotion with some other business: Associate to a sponsor, a competition or promotion and that will make a world of difference for you. For instance, the minimal-sugar candy brand is collaborated with the sugarless Belgian chocolate brand to host a strong engagement present. The concept of this is to obtain strong-quality supporters if you have comparable consumer profiles. Demand that anyone joining the contest accept the message or do a little more secondary practice, like a mark or a follow-up.

2. Reproduce another firms' Material: When you are searching for big follow-up on Instagram, suggest posting content from many other companies in your page. This is indeed a wise and efficient way to expose your company. While adding another company into your posting and endorsing their material, they are probably to return the favor. In certain situations, they will take you away and support your company. Likewise, their fans are likely to have noticed your page. You can only do this individually, or using an app including a repost with Instagram.

3. Give and take Instagram Scream: It is where you tell another company in your sector if they want to share your material or, in exchange, submit theirs. The nice part that you can send and demand different screams. This is a genius Instagram marketing strategy which helps both the company and its sponsors, who are enjoying a huge upswing and reputation.

4. Influencer image: It is a popular strategy that links your company with a prominent figure in your industry. For starters, when you are going to sell with a sportsperson, you could partner with the sportsman or sport enthusiast. This will reveal the business to fans of the influencer when they declare Instagram acquisition throughout the weeks leading up to everything. Through registering with influencer sites, you will identify similar companies and individuals to affiliate. These will be online resources that simplify analyses of exploration, screening, and publishing, allowing you to concentrate more on building influencer partnerships and organizing exciting acquisitions.

5. *Attractive captions:* Most users swipe across their Instagram account while they are lonely and slogging over a basic daily schedule. You will draw and track this community by making interesting Instagram subtitles. The aim is to express the story underlying the videos or photo. If the videos or picture is about a brand, your description is your medium for a short explanation of your piece. Explain why so many people would worry, and try to provide a few updates.

6. *Instagram content:* Ultimately, good comment posts can help shape the company's image and narrative. The aim is to build a copy that promotes interaction, making people know they want what you will be selling. Such techniques offer a quick and efficient way to improve the number of followers. The tests could take a long time if you begin with null followers. This is because nobody knows who you are, so it is difficult to get original fans.

Instagram Apps

Instagram actually provides plenty of powerful tools with filters, but often in a competitive feed, you need some extra motivation to set themselves apart from the other companies. Most Instagram apps are free to support you do that. The best business apps from Instagram will create your comments unforgettable, distinct and worthy. While you may not be capable of attracting all 1 billion customers, you will be capable of attracting those who relate more to your market.

If you should be trying to create better photos, plan updates in preparation, or erase dormant fans, the following are the important features that could be applied for the Instagram advertising toolbox:

1. *Image processing software:* There are really are hundreds of image editor tools to help you polish your photos. Few of our favorites include: Snapseed (iOS and Android) Instagram pictures applications Snapseed's brush feature allows you to set for contrast, color quality, and brightness, that is perfect for scenarios where you do not want to auto-enhance each element in your shot.

VSCO filter is a prominent filter-like filtration and has formatting functions which often trounce Instagram's originality in in-app product lines. Using it to change comparison, improve color, deep edges, and much more. You may change text and unique fonts for your images with such app. It is a chance for you to build a brand buzz and encourage a deal. You also can install video editor software to modify your videos. Using apps including video trim and sound removal, you could build good-looking clips before employing a pro.

2. Apps planning: When you find the right time to comment on Instagram, you could use scheduling tools to build more material for your community. Only add a media object from your mobile collection to Later's portal, as well as the planner will popping up. We also can compose a description, mark the place in which the picture or video was taken, or label other user accounts to maximize the title's discovery.

Video clips and photographs could be posted from Blossom Social's mobile phone app. You can also use other apps, such as a diary that helps you see most of your expected material through social media.

3. Content Applications: In order to get more Instagram followers, you need to distribute content which stand out. This is where performance apps get there.

4. Content Policy of Instagram: One of Instagram's best apps is the Instagram content strategy. The app can be used to add various trendy filters, colors, graphics and models to your posts. Most of the apps are trendy, innovative and are often, influenced by cinematography. Design is a mega-smooth, device-rich photo mixer which immediately shows up to nine photos in different configurations for collage. You can pick and record images of your photo library with both the built-in video simulator when you go.

5. *Video Apps of Instagram:* Splice from GoPro's arrived with basic-yet-powerful authoring tools. To blend your favorite pictures and videos in one coherent media file, you can use this or similar apps to build a creation using the unified music collection and transformation features.

Check these features and use Instagram Ideas to track how these affect your marketing plan. Use those which have positively affected the company along with other social advertising devices. With the availability of amazing apps, here you are bound to find several interesting options.

Conclusion

If we really wish to stay ahead of the game, you could use a method like Later or Buffer to plan automated updates. Instagram tips are indeed conversion tools usable with a company account. This offers you a good insight to your account's main performance indicators, how much publicity the comments get, and to know how committed the consumers are.

We may also observe demographic data about fans, allowing you to reach the intended audience through Instagram. Although this constructed analytics platform is not exhaustive, it is indeed a wonderful tool.

Chapter – 5

YOUTUBE MARKETING

Introduction

YouTube started in 2005 and, expanding rapidly. Each minute, individual around the globe post video footage valued 300 hours on YouTube. YouTube is the world's-largest Web browser, after Google. This ensures that people are regularly looking for information utilizing YouTube and watching videos related to them.

YouTube Videos

YouTube helps users to access any online videos that is posted. YouTube videos contain any subject that anyone wants to upload. Such videos can also be easily shared through other social networks, emails and sites and can be inserted in many other websites.

For any video in YouTube, there is a database of proposed clips. Videos which YouTube's search engine estimates are sure to excite people who are watching it.

YouTube allows users to voice their opinions on content they like, buy clips to read later, and share images they enjoy. You can upload a video accessible to the public or start sharing it with individuals.

YouTube Analytics

YouTube Analytics is indeed a self-service apps and an analysis tool. This provides information of each clip you post, and you can easily control how often viewers have viewed the post, from where people have seen and who have viewed it.

YouTube Channels

You could build up a YouTube channel putting your content together. You can customize your channels with photos reflecting your business. The channel has a tab where you can include a brief overview of your company and a reference to your homepage and contact information. Your network is where you collect the clips you produce and post, the clips you view and like, and the video playlists you build. The channel will also have a Web address (URL) that you might advertise on your blog and other promotional materials. You may connect to your site. It ensures that your clips are shown about your YouTube website once you sign in.

In the YouTube channel, you can still build folders to arrange your videos according to topic or style. For instance, you may have a folder of videos about each one of your product lines, or you may have a playlist submitted by certain consumers to a video contest you manage.

YouTube Promotion

YouTube offers options that allow companies to advertise their content to people who like them, targeting viewers through ages, subjects or preferences. Sponsors pay when someone watches your video. You can still choose the ad that will run, which type of ads, and how often you are willing to pay per display. The YouTube's ad guidance explains the process.

Other Multimedia Providers

Video streaming sites: There are few sources of video streaming sites.

Vimeo: It is a successful video portal with much more professional video makers specializing in it with better quality.

Facebook video manufacturing: It is the most popular social platform, where, Facebook enables users to upload, build and send pictures and images and texts.

Flickr: It is a video sharing network, but it can share content up to minimum 90 seconds.

YouTube Industry and Job opportunity: YouTube is indeed a video search network platform where you can post instructional, exciting and other knowledge clips. In other terms, it is just like a Television, however you can check anything you want to see. YouTube is indeed a Popular video-sharing service located in San Bruno, California. There have been numerous different websites including Vimeo, Metacafe, Veoh, etc. Among these, YouTube is perhaps the most successful video exchanging website.

Features of YouTube

1. *YouTube is indeed a browser:* It is a video-sharing platform, so here we can post videos, we have little to charge for viewing and downloading.

2. *Download or upload clips and photo files:* YouTube has various kinds of videos so you can upload so many clips in either standard like mp4, 3gp, HD 480, or HD 720. To download recording from video, you may search the sound converter for YouTube video from Google.

3. *We can like photos, dislike, download and post:* Such tools are according to the standard and you can like any clip with the like click. But when you so not like an online content, it gives you the chance to dislike. This is because of YouTube's dislike key; it increases the quality and ratings on certain eligible videos. If you really want to make a recommendation, ask the question, want to know about a certain video, so that you can write a comment underneath the clips. You can view a "red color key" to access. That is for fans. Every YouTube use this term in all the posts, when they have more and more followers to the YouTube channel. If you really like the video content, then we can connect it to the site. If video or channel materials are useful to the profession or the industry or to one's personal purpose, you can take subscription to receive email alert whenever that network uploads a new video online.

4. *You can discover any talent you need:* People can obtain knowledge and information from YouTube. For several individuals, YouTube is a learner's forum. Anything is accessible here.

5. *Business learning and network videos:* YouTube has several videos for business learning and network movie outlets to view such clips and training tips and advice could start your own company.

6. *Create your own clips:* People can post any kind of videos for your channel and individuals are watching your videos in various country.

7. *People can share valuable content with others on Facebook, Instagram, Pinterest, Google⁺:* Sharing is conscientious. Whether you like or dislike the video, it is very helpful to someone in their profession and industry. Also, it is nice to share this with colleagues. More users, opinions, and wants will grow and the network will gain attraction and earnings. It is good for the world. Because when we share interesting news, it is a tradition that good people led the world or achieve better stuff.

8. *Make money from the Videos:* People are able to commercialize your clips with Google AdSense. If you really want to make money by monetizing, you could use Google AdSense tools, so you can subscribe for AdSense to your Gmail Password. But before that, to make money, you should provide good tips and fun materials to audiences.

9. The more views you receive, the further you win: If somebody has a good video they are great, and viewers like their clips, you will gain more. YouTube offers you additional advertisements when you have more likes in your posts. You may make fun, instructional, animations, documentary and other useful images.

10. Good quality camera is essential: High-quality clips get more shares, and the viewer is very relaxed. There are free and paid video processing apps on YouTube. Using online video production software, online video development tool people can produce good quality videos.

11. There have been numerous people making good money from advertising: Advertising is a profession for many people. The factors for their success are the experience, excellent communication abilities, sales and business skills.

12. Link your used with others: Individuals may also deal with other people. You can use YouTube's full live streaming service, and link with your user.

13. People can use the Gmail ID using YouTube apps: If you would like to sign up to any YouTube channel, or you like or dislike any video, sign in with just your Gmail ID.

14. It is a way to advertise and support your Company & Products: Any tool may use these times to support your company online and in person, and you cannot overlook. Though YouTube have a better reputation, variety of people use it in different parts of the world and time zones. It will create the opportunity for business owners, suppliers of IT outsourcing products, businessmen to promote their products or services through images, illustrations, demos, etc.

15. Low-cost production and dissemination of instructional educational content: YouTube allows low-cost production and dissemination of instructional educational content and videos produced by independent YouTubers. Worldwide video exposure has fueled creativity, allowing geographically dispersed people to draw on and interact with each other's research.

16. *It can be endorsing harmful contents too:* While YouTube videos conveyed social graces, they also included potentially harmful material. The suggestion algorithm of the website was also shown to promote inappropriate material for children, endorsing potentially dangerous activities.

17. *YouTube is becoming a significant news outlet:* The platform also promoted inters institutional and personal interaction.

Conclusion

YouTube have influenced elections, becoming much more relevant than direct marketing for political advertising. Legislators and policymakers are using the Internet to contact people personally and support policies. YouTube has encouraged freedom via free expression of actual political opinions. The selection system has been used to favor extreme fetishes, contributing to allegations that it has been used as a tool for political radicalization. Large corporations and marketers used the platform as a concentrated resource for digital advertising and consumer development. In addition, individuals have collaborated with brands and have created their own viewers, allowing independent content providers to monetize clips and even gain living standards directly by sharing content.

Chapter – 6

TWITTER MARKETING

Introduction

No one can reject the significance of social network in contemporary society. Brands should be there to create an impact and effects. Application of social media thus are improving day by day. Two billion of the globe's population out of 7 billion use social networks. Hence, a business enterprise cannot ignore it. A successful online presence should function for your company. People can use Twitter to achieve their goals, formulate their views and earn revenue in various ways.

Business Strategy by Twitter

1. Introduce Twitter Cards: You choose Twitter cards to show any message you receive. Twitter cards is a wonderful way of choose and receive the tweets. You can organize the page and guarantee that when people are sharing the messages, the picture appears in the tweets when the people submit.

2. Help your company grow: If you create the Twitter Followers properly and the followers are committed and well-targeted, you can help your company to grow. Social Quant is a platform that easily improves the related Twitter followers by using analytics to find appropriate people and exchanges. When the number of followers grows, you will get much more exposure and visits for your site.

3. *Recognize Influencers and Connect with them:* Until you connect with influencers and you cannot create an opportunity to obtain more fans, more exposure and more ad impressions. If someone affects your industry, they had the exposure you need. Creating good partnerships and it can add more value. With Social connection, you could easily find such influencers.

4. *Use Twitter addresses to handle your connections:* As you follow larger numbers, your time line may feel overwhelming. When there are others you would really like to keep a record of and their messages you do not want to skip, link everyone to a Twitter list or monitor the regular account alongside. Tools such as HootSuite and TweetDeck enable you to literally set pages to follow tweets of your profiles.

5. *Using Twitter Advertisements to Target the Email:* Recording your mailing list includes people who choose to know more about you, so they are wonderful people to identify to your advertisements. People can Customize Audiences to configure the advertising and access your email list. Twitter matches and targets the emails with active users if you have anything to advertise.

6. *Right Hashtags:* Tweets with one or two hashtags are greater than those who have even more. It may be appealing to cram every hashtag that you might know of into a message to draw attention but this seems to be rather negative.

7. *Study Your Competing products:* Viewers Choose to discover out whether your rivals are also on Twitter. Utilizing Twitonomy, you could join any Twitter username as well as obtain comprehensive profile analysis. That's what my profile shows. You could see information of how often I comment and some of the individuals I pursue, who adopted me home.

8. *Search Twitter to Keyword:* Instruments like HootSuite and TweetDeck allow consumers set up query columns to instantly illustrate any reference of a specific set of words. For starters, let us assume you run a business and still want to identify people searching for great food in your city. It may want to find the words like "health tips" or "where and how to eat" or list the major city. First, checkup and pay attention to tweets. Build interactions and connections. For whichever your company you are looking for use both the keywords you are searching for when you are seeking help. Browse for and react positively.

9. *Configuration of UTM Monitoring*: UTM monitoring may sound a little bit difficult. And once it is set up, it is a great way of tracking and evaluating any connections you pass. UTM monitoring adds extra information to connect you to discuss. So that you can track where consumers are clicking and what occurred after they scrolled. To begin with UTM monitoring, make unique URLs of each reference you post online. Analytics may not figure to see which clicks came from either the Twitter ad and which come by your other posts. It is impossible to monitor modifications, splash rates, and purchases. UTM monitoring solves this issue by developing personal URLs for each link, so that you can add information as to whether a connection is from remunerated or for natural traffic.

10. *Use the Pinned Tweet*: Twitter permits the user to pin one twitter post atop of the schedule. When anyone opens the profile, first they may get to see the tweet. This means that they cannot see your spontaneous tweet. Alternatively, they will get the most significant message you have picked. Pinned tweets are a good way to highlight your new marketing or latest material. Tap on both the three dots within a change and choose. Add to your account page.

11. *Using Good Headlines*: When people search your account, with more convincing headlines you can motivate them. Talk of creative titles for your posts or blog posts. The Psychological Marketing Quality Headline Analyzer offers you a ranking for each title. It can help you identify the right word mix of effects.

12. *Twitter Analytics to examine and simplify*: Twitter Analytics to show you, how often views or how much involvement your tweets are getting. Going through the metrics in depth, you will discover what your crowd reacts to most. You have to continually develop your level of commitment. Learning the analytics may assist you to improve the account.

Methods to Introduce and Renewed Business for Your Twitter Endeavors

1. Organize to Track: Organize the lists to track other people on Twitter for commercial reasons like clients, vendors, rival companies, colleagues or rivals. When the number of followers increases, it shows that the activities are becoming effective and the positive messages between all others are developing.

Twitter profiles are its most influential factor. Profiles enable to cluster the individuals that a person pursue and they do not get destroyed in everyone's noise.

By developing or using Twitter addresses, you can concentrate on tweets from different segments or group and determine when and how to interact with them. So, do not destroy the comments from significant people.

One can produce minimum up to 20 Twitter addresses group and each of which has up to 500 accounts. It may track each database independently utilizing Twitter.com and HootSuite software.

2. Build an interaction list: It defines your everyday Twitter interaction. When you follow an individual who motivates you, people who say creative ideas, pushing you to feel differently then, Twitter will become a delight.

Building a personal conversation page is a good way to reflect on the individuals who motivate you without forgetting anybody in the group.

This interaction group may include: Individuals who encourage you and who motivate you individually in the business and personal life. People who speak fun with great example. A discussion list enables to reduce time by bringing together a more influential people and discussions in to a single collection.

Make the list open and personal. By making a private list, you are the only person who understands who was on your roster, and when you're changing. Conversation to other people on just this page, however, remains public. So, watch your tongue.

3. *Edit the profile image:* The image appears in front of every submitted message. It is an occasion to connect an image with the business to identify the company.

The Twitter profile photo should be unique. The emblem has to be in best shape or size. It must reflect the company and business properly.

The business should have a beautiful logo and it must lead to success in business. The image is the icon of business. Ensure the logo matches and look respectful, creating the impression that specifically applies to your company.

Keep the icon visible. If the logo includes things which people cannot understand, it will create confusion and monotony. Create a logo without words and one that catches the logo's meaning.

Consumers relate with images, not with the icons. If images are the main driver of the business, why not just use images and make the company more ethical and accessible.

Focus in the face. Individuals do not want the brand on the seaside, and they do not care unnecessary elements.

No animals or children are used even though your company is directly linked to animals or kids. The image should be centered and choose to communicate with prospective customers.

Whereas a skilled photograph is best, use a camera to capture a good shot. Ensure the shot not on a dark background. Start taking more shots to choose the best.

Learn Best Inbound Marketing Strategies from top Experts of the globe. Try to tracking up with key patterns and knowing exactly how to execute the new strategies effectively.

If you do not have the ability to change the brand image or frame ask the person or hire a designer for this. The modest work will pay dividends down the road to Twitter's technical footprint.

4. *Transform the Twitter graphical branding:* Personalize the Twitter profile page's glance and color schemes. It gives the chance to provide additional sales and may offer details to anyone who reviews the account. Try to make custom graphics for your Twitter history.

After creating the picture file, publish it to the profile. Here, the company can may modify context and connect colors to organize with your new wallpaper image. To suit the context and references, there need to have good protocols for the shades in your picture.

5. *Revise the biography of the Twitter profile:* The unique Twitter profile bio tells the narrative through a message and loads of information for just a few phrases. A best Twitter status includes other elements: tell people what you are doing, understand how you are helping kids, and show that you have the required personality through a good bio as an example. A best Twitter bio illustrates what you are doing and also, demonstrates your character. Reframe it so that it informs potential buyers and assist them and how they might benefit from linking with you. Study and upgrade your Twitter profile every six months and label your schedule. The best bio brings good business over a period of time.

6. *Consider developing a Twitter homepage:* Many people use their Twitter website link to write people off at their front door or blog. So, you can build a special Twitter homepage and use that as your Twitter domain name.

A Twitter homepage provides you further platform to talk about the business and your Twitter usage. A Twitter homepage is a unique page on your site designed to teach people from Twitter about your company. It is like getting a well-wisher to help individuals to have the scoop in your company and then, use Twitter.

Twitter homepage may include a private message by you, the information about your company goods and services such as, how to be a consumer? Why do you tweet about individuals inside your Twitter account? Etc. Although you have more possibility, keep your Twitter homepage brief and to-the-point to offer your guests a big impression.

7. Reconsider the follow-up plan: Most Twitter accounts do not have real people. Bots are automatically generated applications and some are hackers.

There have been bots that bring useful data. Some bots distribute messages from other users and other websites that are not promoting the Twitter business objectives. Try to block these kinds of feed which provide no business performance. Perhaps, the person may not know that you followed a bot. Bots achieve a crowd by following other users and taking advantage of people who naturally follow back. Basically, if you really want to stop your Twitter stream loading up with trash, it is best not to follow anyone who mentions you. For instance, troll Bots typically have small numbers, followed by large numbers.

But, how one can detect a bot, spammer, or anyone whom you should not follow back? When they have not disturbed uploading an actual profile, they are unlikely to say anything worth saying.

By checking the numbers one can understand a spammer. The spammer may accompany many individuals, but may have only few supporters. By analyzing the tweets one can understand spammer. If several users receive the precise tweet over a very short period of time it is likely a bot. No absolute favorites list or twitter posts. A bot or spammer may not favor messages or generate lists.

8. *Listen closely and follow:* Social networks is about discussions, and conversations mean you are talking and listening. You may pay attention on Twitter by Writing tweets. That is the key to finding your Twitter group's brains. Seek answers and cites. Each time you update Facebook, you must first search for private messages or discusses. References are social communications which include your Twitter treatment and direct messages sent specifically to you.

Scan for your brand name. Often people discuss your brand without the use of your Twitter name. So, you must check Twitter frequently for people who suggest your title by developing and sparing a search. You must follow whoever speaks on Twitter. So that, when you find other people speaking for you or about the company, you can pursue them.

Train Digital marketing Expert!

Try to be front of your rivals and essential to have a social media expert. Learn how to boost the Digital marketing in online media platform. You can mingle with major social media initials and products, absorb numerous tips and strategies, and enjoy comprehensive opportunities.

9. *Promote the twitter account:* Allow the people to locate your company on Facebook by linking the Twitter name to all your company products. Easily join your company on Twitter by adding a Twitter Follow key on your professional website may increase the marketing. For instance, in such locations you must offer your Twitter username: your web site, the email fingerprint and your email list with a link. Your company cards Indications posted into your business documentation you offer customers menu options and consumer information sheets.

10. *Be sure you read your clients:* Twitter is a good platform to discuss to consumers. Nevertheless, it implies that you need to communicate to them. You cannot be sure of which of the users are your clients on Twitter. That is why it is essential to promote your Twitter feed to your clients and then the clients can consider you.

The way of information to your Twitter consumer is important. Few consumers may begin a chat by exhausting the Twitter. You must track whoever dialogues for your corporate. They are naming your company. Arrange a recovered search on Twitter to find the people speaking of your business. Always answer and look at people who cite your company. You may also search your clients using your email book's email address.

11. *Ignore inactive individuals:* Do not waste times who are trying to regulate or who are inactive. Pruning the people who prevented using Twitter is a great idea. An excellent free resource to meet people that have not posted a little while is unTweeps. This lets you create a chart of your supporters depending on how soon since their first post. You can make a list of websites you visit based on the number of weeks after their last tweet. Focus on people that have not tweeted six weeks and update the chart. You can unfold personal accounts. When you have a great number of consumers who are no matter how long post, do not pursue them all together. Such intervention may signify Twitter's removal of offensive and spammer-like conduct.

12. *Place Twitter to seek to solve your company difficulties:* Sometime the way to improve your knowledge is to inquire more. If you were using Twitter passively, causing the events to happen, perhaps it is time to give Twitter a better task.

Use twitter, though it takes a few times before you are ready to work on your business objectives. But once you have learned Twitter and created a group, it is time to bring your Twitter to the next level. Twitter will help you achieve your objectives. Consider the contemporary business challenge. There are ways to solve the problem by Twitter. For Example; provide a Twitter-only offer. Offer a special deal for anyone who knows the secret code you tweet at 5 pm on Tuesday.

Honor all who retweet you. It brings your profile really dynamic. Twitter is a great blog traffic moving device. Arranged a competition or bonus for users retweeting your blog entries. You may give an audiobook, a seat for game, a free consultation, or a consumer refund. Clarify the terminology of the request into your tweet in a blog or on a special website page such that people realize your request.

13. Incorporate photograph with the messages: People enjoy photos. Social networking sites has extended more to this and have given them more. Figures show that if you include more pictures, individuals usually read more of your stuff online. This ensures that by just including images to your messages, you will significantly increase their interest. Incorporating a picture to your Twitter post increases the number of individuals to your text.

The greatest factor seems to be that the images need not be of competent-quality to be successful on Twitter. Use your digital camera to snap a photo. One can also use the device's Twitter mobile app to twitter post and compile your image.

14. You could save crucial tweets: However, as portion of their Twitter approach, many companies use the Favorites and important tweets. Use your Web browser photo sharing tool or an Internet-based screenshotting product like Delicious to bookmark essential tweets. So, you have a way of keeping monitor of essential tweets for long term use.

15. Broaden the Twitter exchange for the blog: When you have a good brief exchange or if you discover a topic people are reacting to on Twitter there is a possibility to broaden the discussion to people who are reading your website. Twitter today makes it much easier for you to put a Twitter post in a blog, so it makes it look like a Twitter post and has the same interactive elements on Twitter. In many other terms, publish a blog.

Conclusion

Analysis (and renew) your tweet subjects. For a while, most companies start utilizing Twitter. People sometimes post on random subjects, or do not post very often since they do not know what else to say. After learning the essentials of Twitter's reply types and constructing your Web community, this is time to take your topics of conversation seriously.

Or, use branding jargon to build a digital strategy. Each company has a primary focus around its goods and services. Those things you think about your company, and things your clients and online forum wants to understand from you. You sometimes educate clients about such topics.

Most companies struggled to find them as they accept their information for given. With some attempt, you can start seeing your business skills into your customers' eyes and find out subjects who really garner interest in your society. Those are the issues to concentrate on with Twitter and digital media in general. When you have a website, this should be your website classifications.

Chapter – 7

INTERACTIVE MARKETING

Introduction

Interactive marketing is also known as event driven marketing and is a business strategy that utilizes two-way communication networks to directly link customers to a business. Even though this interaction can take place in real life, it has happened entirely online via email, social networks, and forums over the last decade.

Since 1995, online marketing has been seen as potential of e-marketing and electronic advertisement. Around 1997, the Review of Direct Advertising was re-branded as the Review of Online Marketing, which exists today. Salesforce.com was created in 1999, enabling advertisers and salesmen to directly impact and motivate potential clients through marketing of the product.

With the introduction of digital marketing in the early 1990s, and HubSpot's founding in 2006, functionality has seen a paradigm shift from easy two-way interaction to gamification and even beyond. The above specific type of customizable marketing is recognized as interactive digital marketing, and several firms were established to react to the use of new content types and market leader differentiation.

Applications

As collaborative advertising depends on getting a medium of communication with customers, social media platforms were a big part of this approach, probably led by advertising or consumer achievement agencies. Interactive branding has been most commonly used as a trend setter in sales and marketing. Interactive marketing has been almost closely linked to digital marketing, so businesses can generate multiple-shared, viewer-relevant content, or "goes viral," and finally create themselves as just a power in their sector. Customers generally trust certain specific rulers in their sector, so this approach can take in several inbound tends to lead.

Participative Marketing

Interactive marketing often regarded as "experiential marketing," "event branding," "on-ground marketing," "living marketing," "involvement marketing," "commitment marketing" or "social events marketing". It is a business strategy that specifically participates and encourages customers to engage in the natural selection of a product or brand understanding. Instead of seeing customers as inactive recipients of advertisements, interaction advertisers claim customers should be personally involved in creating and co-creating advertising campaigns, building a partnership with the brand.

Client Involvement happens when a label and a customer connect. Actually, conceptual advertising is real, one-on-one experiences enabling customers to engage with products. Customers will seek and expect one-on-one, reciprocal customer engagement.

Virtual Expansion

Experiential advertising is a rising trend involving the selling of a good or service through interactions that attract consumers and build passionate relationship to the product/service. Material and collaborative experiences strengthen a consumer's offer for a product and convert clients as they are the part of them. Involvements and experiences are positively linked to client perceptions, temperament and habits. They also constitute a way a business can obtain competitive edge by distinguishing itself against rivals. An interaction should be entertaining, convincing and worthy of stimulating the perceptions of the consumer and winning his/her allegiance.

Some factors separate conventional from the experiential branding. Primarily, experiential advertising relies on delivering customer physical, psychological, mental and moral principles. Secondly, experiential advertising aims at building synergies around context, understanding, use, and customer loyalty. Moreover, experiential marketing involves more varied research methodology to know consumers.

There are six-step processes to establish active marketing strategies. The first phase involves a user experience assessment to evaluate the product's actual experience. The second option is to build a product network and consumer touchstone. The subsequent phase involves planning the customer experience; organizing staff, goods, and systems against both the product proposal. The next phases involve discussing the product idea internal and external. This last phase is quality management to ensure the company fulfills its targets.

Experiential advertising becomes quickly technologically sophisticated and customized. The large Internet reach and increased competition between online stores has led to the rise of digital experiential marketing. Utilizing audio and visual resources, it uses social media and its multiple platforms to construct enhanced and immersive content. This focuses on a digital atmosphere that participates clients to develop an unprecedented knowledge and thus recreate their loyalty. Components characterizing digital reality advertising are: feeling, communication, enjoyment, motion, and group connection. Thereby, the customer experience should highlight a customer's emotional argument to construct buyback intention.

A Digital Consumer Experience Method

The company has to create a convincing consumer-value plan. It really is important to know whether a shopping experience will meet consumer needs.

Production of the virtual user experience structure to resolve all areas of customer-business communication is important.

Maximize the use of "7Cs" to endorse the structure. Material, flexibility, customer service, collaboration, culture, networking and usability are main resources for the framework.

Incorporate consumer experience online and offline. Businesses can greatly enhance the digital customer satisfaction through accurate of offline world links.

Commitment measures to what degree a customer has constructive brand knowledge when subjected to advertising, sponsorship, broadcasting contact or any other knowledge. In March 2006, the Marketing Research Foundation (ARF) described "interaction" as transforming towards a brand concept improved by the contextual cues. The ARF also described the purpose by which involvement affects a product as:

Multi-dimensional transfer

In 2009, Keith Ferrazzi reported that perhaps the Digital age is turning in with what he called as the Relationship Age, "in which passion, sensitivity and teamwork are essential characteristics of achievement" and where "software and interaction collide and confidence, dialogue and partnership are high on the agenda. Three-dimensional involvement (3DE)" has "not only length, but depth, in which both the donor and the transmitter communicate to a higher authority and the experience is altered, not only a discussion, but a relationship to an intent that converts everything in the system."

The key point of difference between interaction marketing and other types is that the latter is driven by an ideology instead of a focus on individual marketing tools. The concept is that audiences should be included in the selling process whenever they want and by any means they choose.

Offline Promotion Tools

General advertising, often recognized as general teams. Teen marketing, often known as enjoyment marketing. Event management, is also recognized as event marketing. In Brand marketing rides sometimes, marketers will be using customized programmers, buses or vehicles to attract attention to their product, acting as brand advertisements or mobile hubs to build customer encounters on-site in commercial parking garages or in industrial parking lots.

Corporations encourage their brands via virtual reality marketing via facilities such as charging points. IOT Machine linked to social networks showing off-line clients fan figures and personalized texts. Interactive narrative utilizes simulation and interactive technology to build virtual reality for user interaction. Brands can communicate with their customers in new and innovative ways utilizing software such as digital or virtual reality, CGI and 360° video content, facial and motion detection, holographic and ultra-haptics, 3D scanning, maps, printing, handheld and mobile systems, remote sensing-location techniques, robots, photo booths as well as magical hands.

Online Marketing Method

Blogs: Organizations may share material of their own blogs for interaction purposes or service providers on similar public blogs. Hosting a promotion that rewards external blogs followers for their interest in some kind of competition is an instance of an internal blogs interaction marketing campaign.

Social media sites: social media sites such as Facebook, LinkedIn, and Twitter are perfect for consumer interaction as they provide a way for users to connect with the products and build a conversation with the consumers and the businesses. Many businesses have coverage on many of these pages. Most of these sites have provided particular types of online company followings. For starters, Facebook launched fan pages. Engagement effects such as communication habits involve motives like satisfaction, self-efficacy, education, financial gain, altruism, compassion, social engagement, consumer interest, mutuality, and credibility and social reactions to fan pages. It signals social interaction importance, marked object's general appearance and personality attraction.

Webcasts: Unlike private Webcast conferences with a limited, restricted invite list, digital content advertising activities reach a much greater public audience. These are usually on-demand or online, enabling users to watch content of their own time. Same as to conferences, throughout live streams, members of the audience will ask to participants questions and vote in surveys.

Email campaigns: It is one of the first digital marketing methods. E-mail marketing allows target groups to opt-in specifically and receive messages from a marketing company. Companies may also promote people to virtually discuss their texts by emailing colleagues, friends, and family.

Crowdsourcing: crowdsourcing services offer business opportunities via open media competitions. Such crowdsourcing platforms create brand ambassadors as just a natural result of the crowdsourcing system itself through enabling users to create their entries on different social networks.

Interactive Ads

Digital marketing is the aspect of digital advertising that utilizes virtual online or offline platforms to engage with customers and sell products, brands, services or ads, business and activist groups. It is most usually done online and often using an ad client that can produce a range of immersive marketing units.

1. Purpose

Interactive marketing targets typically match traditional marketing objectives, i.e. selling a product. In turn it implies that most of the traditional marketing impact and usefulness elements stay relevant, within interactive entertainment scope. Nevertheless, as per Interactive Marketing approach interactive advertising has some resources that extend the variety of potential targets and boost marketing efficiency. Interactive marketing has the ability to reduce casualties connected with uncoordinated advertisements, reduce common difficulties in communicating a marketing signal and help to overcome product hurdles.

2. Advantages

Interactive marketing allows audiences to view ads in different ways which interpretations, and demonstrates the growing importance of the involvement of the customer in calculating the cost of campaigns in contemporary society. Digital advertising invites users to actively participate in corporate communications itself and provide suggestions, ignore insignificant components.

As commercialism is becoming more popular in the worldwide economy and political interactions are becoming more important in creating sustainable lengthy-term relationships with customers. Interactive advertising is also becoming more important as it activates greater incentive for socialization around potential customers and distributors.

3. The drawbacks

While interactive marketing might be strongly attractive to a formulated viewer, preparation is hard, expensive and moment-consuming, particularly for market segments that need to be correctly recognized and examined.

Interactive marketing results in markets where imagination can catch consumers' interest. Furthermore, there is very little space for it in some markets, and increased use of creative thinking can be a form of sound that affects delivering desired texts to customers.

4. Elements

Interactive marketing has several aspects, such as differing techniques and kinds. Using various types of behavioral techniques and marketing strategies, with such ads, companies may maximize the effectiveness of their promotions. All advertising can be categorized into five categories, such as brand and provider, advertising, difficulty, commercial and economic. Advertising styles often communicate with the intentions of the client to manipulate events and customer reactions, highlighting the need for digital ads as a way to persuade potential customers or target markets.

Using the Web as the primary device for interactive marketing to research the systems, styles and results, we can look out for various aspects governed by users or advertisers.

Processes, Internet intentions, and style are key customer-controlled variables. Hence, some scholars and professionals suggest that users had more Internet power than marketers. Others have argued that immersive advertising and marketing methods will not operate unless professionals "step into the shoes" and understand the Web from the consumer's perspective.

5. Marketer reviewed facets

Marketer controls different aspects of online advertising. Many of these factors involve structural components, including ad kinds, browsers, and characteristics. This does not mean customers never regulate immersive ads framework. Definitions for audience-controlled online advertisements include display advertisement, advertising, web links and multi-carrier sites.

Virtual Communication

The advertising landscape as well as customer relationship management is constantly evolving. Digital advertising is the latest update, among the most thrilling. The digital world provides the company the chance to either succeed in the market or drop underneath ever-changing times. Facebook itself has millions of monthly users creating a virtual network where advertisers can interact and engage to consumers in ways that has never been. We may define their interests, customize their ads, and create alternative interactions and correspondence. They can notify someone about the firm's lived experience, beneficial or harmful. The success of this will be shown with Trip Advisor, which, based on user reviews, has become the first request for flight information and affecting travel operator's industry in both positive and negative.

This digital platform could be used by companies for the benefit of the customers. We can probably build digital customer groups and customer loyalty. What companies connect in the virtual environment becomes increasingly relevant as their product represents. Answering the questions and coping with criticisms rapidly is essential and a simple way to end digital marketing. As these digital platforms are quite public, it renders how companies cope with customers a rather sensitive matter, as a terrible feeling affects not only primary customer, but anyone that occurs to see it. A negative examination or comment could significantly affect future income on organizations.

Customers seem to be more comfortable when visiting the online markets as they are at home and at ease and relaxed. Consumers incline not to be less conscious of the range of marketing strategies employed while in the actual marketplace. Marketing companies aim this as decisions are made freer and much more happily. The online model allows the public to order immediately, instead of go to a real shop. No physical bill makes it much easier for the customer not to realize the cash they only spent. Today Digital retail is a simple and easy purchase model and deals for many consumers.

The online market depends on brand images, meaning the colors as well as how the item appears and differ from the digital product. Such images are changed using Photoshop to make them more consumer-friendly. This is a downside because customers still have to experience, view and sample the brand until reaching a purchase decision. Companies have to be present in both ways such as physical and digital. The digital marketing is progressively becoming the major marketing forum with virtual practical support. Whereas, it was in the inverse order in the last decade.

1. *Social Media Implementation*

Marketers use this digital medium as a way to market to customers especially social networks, such as Facebook Twitter and Instagram. Social networking helps to categorize users by allowing communities to meet, defining their desires. Companies now have an auto-selected product differentiation and their they can focus their ads. Companies can use digital interaction as a way of contacting customers and get information, business insights and interaction, as well as provide the information they may need before making a purchase. Such online interaction helps the customer to create a feeling of' relationship with the company as they are able to communicate and chat effortlessly with them, building confidence and customer loyalty. One method a company uses through virtual world is conducting games over social networks or take advantage of its availability. These contests are used to obtain more supporters: "like or even share this comment". With "want and discuss this post". Companies have become progressively imaginative to maximize efficiency and advantages. For starters, when National Geographic launched their contest, my NatGeo cover image, they challenged people to submit their own pictures they had made, include a picture, and still be in to win. This movement also gives the customer a sense of being a National Geographic artist, but also offered National Geographic a lot of information regarding their clients and their visiting behaviors, picture methods and more.

Social networking was a groundbreaking business strategy for many businesses sector. Tourism, for example, once controlled by airlines and travel leaflets now dominates Internet forums and reserving sites. Tourism industry gets an easy forum to post pictures to motivate and generate consumers. Give customers data about locations to go and where and how to stay, even when traveling through effective marketing techniques can be used to help consumers to recall their stint there. Companies can choose either paid ads or uncompensated social networking sites commercials. Also unpaid, organization and companies run contests for their marketing. Paid is where company pays the social media website to display its advertising on the customers screen without the user's consent. Those are typically on the display side or "supported," depends entirely about what the company pays.

Role in Organizations

Companies' Online interaction is also fresh for corporations, but they see the potential to assess the returns on marketing expenditure in the virtual environment. Kumar, Bezawada, Rishika, Janakiraman and Kannan (2016) commissioned a research to decide the impacts on customers of marketing and advertising. The results revealed that social media marketing is efficient, even though it is more efficient if cross-channel advertisements are being used. Cross-channel marketing when a company tries to sell on various channels, such as social networking sites or publications. Few scholars suggest that executive's use of social networking is a way for further communicating with client and helping to create a greater connection. It will help to grow brand awareness and boost consumer purchases. It is proposed that executives engage in marketing and advertising, although they are reluctant about the calculation since specific effects are not yet apparent. It is known that social networking marketing is much more likely to boost brand image and build customer loyalty than revenue on a brand. It is because the customer might not need or need the original product, but they will still see the brand and then become intimately acquainted with it.

Conclusion

Old marketing tactics are no longer appropriate for contemporary society, though the Internet age is sweeping over and changing the way of advertiser's approach to customers. While advertising previously concentrated on the item, it is now much better to focus on the customer and the product itself. Companies cannot really expect to interact as they were and where they post pictures or brand descriptions. They will update their advertising strategy to satisfy online customer needs. IT raises the question as to whether companies ought to be able to publish on social networks, a way to reach colleagues and use as a means of leisure. In these sites, company ads could be seen as invasive, or violation of privacy or even immoral. This might affect the company's brand. Hence, clients usually accept that social networks are business which needs support for their channels. So, we acknowledge that marketing is the way systems are financed and acknowledge it as necessary. So that, it does not mean that customers may not experience the repetitive or intrusive ads, which may in turn affect mutuality to the advertisement and harm their product relation. Nonetheless, the question reminds the companies that they must value the platforms as a space of same level discussions and personal recreation and ensure that their participation in these platforms is not patronizing or invasive.

Chapter – 8

MOBILE MARKETING

Mobile advertising is a dual-channel digital marketing strategy centered on targeting a particular audience via devices, phones, laptops or other similar apps via blogs, SMS or MMS, email, social media and mobile apps. Mobile marketing may provide consumers with time-sensitive, customized personal data, promoting goods, facilities, consultation alerts and concepts. Theoretically, scholar Andreas Kaplan describes mobile marketing as "any marketing exercise performed across an omnipresent system in which customers are continuously attached via a personal cell instrument". Short Message Service (SMS) advertising had become progressively popular in Europe and parts of Asia in the late 2000s when companies began collecting cell phone numbers as well as sending out desired material. Typically, Text messages get an accessible rate of 98 percent but are read inside three seconds, make it highly efficient to attain beneficiaries quickly.

In recent years, SMS advertising is becoming a valid promotional channel in the globe. That is because, contrast to Internet messaging, providers who control their own infrastructure have set standards and methodologies for the digital media business. The Interactive Advertising Bureau (IAB as well as the Mobile Marketing Association (MMA) also set standards and evangelize marketers' utility of the cell phone channel. Although this has been productive in developed areas like North America, Europe and other nations, mobile Spam mails continue to be a problem in several other places around the world, due to transporters trying to sell their signatory data bases to private entities. In India, though, policy attempts to create National Do Not Call Registry supported mobile consumers to avoid SMS advertising by submitting a quick SMS and calling 1909.

Mobile SMS advertising methods have increased rapidly in Asia and Europe as a main channel to approach consumers. Originally, SMS attracted negative press in many European countries as a particular form of advertising as some marketers bought lists and then sent unrequested messages to customers' phones. But, as regulations were implemented by mobile networks, SMS is the most common division of the digital advertising industry with many 100 million promotional SMS sent monthly to Europe alone. That is because Text messages are technology irreligious and they can be sent to almost every cell phone, tablet, or camera phone or received without Wi-Fi or cellular data link. This may be worth noting as there will be over 5.5 billion distinctive mobile active users worldwide in 2018, about 66 percent of the world population.

SMS promotion have inbound and outbound marketing programs. Inbound marketing relies on progressive production., and outbound marketing relies on sending text messages for purchases, ads, tournaments, gifts, participation on television programs, commitment and remembering activities.

Main Elements of SMS Marketing

1. Provider ID: A transmitter ID is indeed the name or numbers representing the source. Digital numbers, short codes, and special titles are most widely used for commercial purposes and can be rented by bulk SMS companies.

2. Exchanged digital numbers: As the title suggests, many recipients exchange digital numbers. They are generally free, but they cannot get SMS responses, as well as the switching without notification or approval. Senders might have distinct joint digital numbers on various ways, which may be misleading or unreliable probably depends on the situation. For e.g.: mutual digital numbers may be ideal for two step verification text messages, since receivers frequently anticipate such messages, often prompted by sender behavior. However, for messages the beneficiary does not expect, like a marketing advancement, a profound digital number might be chosen.

3. Codes: Short codes suggest very comparable to a devoted digital number, but who are brief mobile figures, typically five to six digits. Their duration and accessibility vary in each country. These will be generally expensive and are used by corporations or government organizations. In mass communications, short codes are chosen to a designated digital number due to their higher production and are good in time-sensitive promotions or for emergency situation.

In the past decades, cellphones short codes are utilized increasingly common as a main channel to connect with mobile customers. Brands has started to view the short SMS code as a digital domain enabling users to send text messages to the product at a case, in shop, as well as off the conventional media.

4. *Transmitter ID*: A customized user ID, commonly defined as a numeric user ID, allows users to change a business address as sender ID of one-way communications organization-to-consumer. This will only be backed in some nations and is up to 11 digits long, and supports bottom-case and lower Senders are not permitted to use numbers only as this would imitate a short code or digital number not accessed. Appropriate bulk SMS companies must pre-check consumer recipient IDs to ensure senders do not exploit or manipulate them.

5. *Length of the message*: The message length would specify the number of Text messages sent, determining the amount spent on advertising a products or services. Not that all text letters are same length.

A single SMS text is approx. 1120 bits. This is critical because there are two forms of encoding, GSM and Unicode. Latin languages and English are GSM-based encoding, 7 bits per line. Typically, text messages get

Mobile Marketing | 79

their 160 character per SMS maximum. Large messages beyond this cap are interrelated. They are split into smaller messages recombined by the receiving phone.

Interconnected messages fit 153 characters instead of 160. A text of 177 characters is sent as two packets. The first is sent with 153 characters, the second with 24. For most bulk SMS providers, the SMS concatenation cycle can occur up to four times, giving senders a limit of 612-character message per project.

Non-Latin languages such as Chinese and emojis use a specific encoding process known as Unicode and UTF-8. It is intended to cover all performance characters, but has a limitation. Every Unicode symbol is 16 bits in length, allowing more data to send, restricting text messages to 70 letters. Messages spanning 70 characters are concatenated. Such messages can match 67 characters and can be concatenated up to four times for 268 characters.

6. *Frame work of the content:* Unique components which can be positioned in a text message include: 1). UTF-8 letters: send SMS in various languages, numbers and symbols. 2). Key words: use keywords to activate an automated email. 3). Links: readily track initiatives using abbreviated URLs to design product pages. 4). Animated elements: images, graphics, video, or audio. 5). Texting is modest, but when it came to SMS advertising. Common messaging forms include notifications, notes, phrases and Multimedia Messaging (MMS) systems.

7. *SMS Marketing alerts:* Sale warnings are most elementary form SMS promotion. Typically used in the registration, daily deals, and special offers. Standard communications contain discount codes and additional details including expiry dates, goods, and links.

8. *SMS Notifications:* Notifications are widely utilized only for appointment based or periodic activities. Several recipients want to ask their beneficiaries to react with a SMS key word to verify their meeting. It can help to increase the sender's business processes and decrease missed appointments, leading to greater efficiency and income.

9. Spam's regulation: Same as to email SMS has country-by-country anti-spam rules. In particular, it is necessary to acquire the receiver's consent before transmitting any SMS, particularly a message form of SMS advertising. Approval can be acquired in a variety of ways, such as enabling opportunities or clients to: tick a website authorization button, fill out a form, or get written agreement.

In many other countries, SMS transmitters must recognize as their website address within their original text message. Identity could be placed either in the recipient ID or the reply copy. Spam protection regulations can also refer for SMS marketing campaigns, which should include an opt-out form.

The primary criteria is that the user opts in to the product. Wireless carriers request double swap-in from the customer and the right of the user to sign up-out at any time by transmitting the term STOP via SMS.

10. ON-NET Routing: ON-NET networking is international messaging's very common form. This is the most secure and convenient route for telecom/providers to receive data, since they receive emails specifically from either the bulk SMS network. For senders needing accuracy and performance, it must be recommended to locate a supplier utilizing ON-NET routing.

11. Gray routing: Grey Routing is a concept for texts sent to providers via low-cost interconnection contracts with the other providers. Rather than sending the email specifically to the desired carrier, several bulk SMS services are sent into an overseas carrier to relay the signal to the desired carrier. The roundabout is easier at the expense of continuity and performance, and these paths can vanish without warning and are faster. Most providers do not like this form of filtering, but they often obstruct it with filtering in the SMSCs.

12. Rout mixing: Many bulk SMS services may integrate more efficient gray configuration on reduced-value networks with their ON-NET offerings. When well controlled routes, texts can be produced efficiently. Hybrid routing considered much more popular for SMS messages where promptness and efficient transmission are less troublesome.

Elements of Mobile Marketing

SMS Package Suppliers

A bulk SMS provider is the simplest and most effective way to send SMS advertising campaign. Typically, innovation and grade SMS services enable new clients to sign up for free trial consideration before executing to their model. Additionally, large companies offer free spam enforcement, actual-time reporting, connection tracking, various implementation solutions, and 100 percent distribution guarantee. Many vendors could provide connection shorter and constructed-in metrics to monitor that campaign's return on investment.

Text message could pay a just feel cents that depends entirely on the provider and state. Senders planning to give lots of messages monthly or yearly may receive rebates from providers.

Even though spam law varies from nation to nation, SMS services are typically site-specific. It is a list for each continent's most common and reliable SMS businesses, with some information on the number of devices in use. It really is important to remember that text pricing, message passing and product offerings will also vary significantly from nation to nation.

MMS (Multimedia Message Service)

MMS mobile advertising can produce timed picture, message, video and audio slideshows. This Content is transmitted through MMS. Practically all new devices with such a color screen can transmit normal

MMS message. Brands can submit and obtain rich content to portable subscribers via MMS.

A standard GSM-based MMS text might have up to 1,500 letters, while Unicode-based messages may have limited to 500 letters. Messages that are shorter than the cap are overwritten and not comma separated as SMS.

App-Based Marketing

The strong economic growth of mobile use has already significantly increased the data usage. In the past couple of years, the number of active downloads has increased exponentially, with billions of downloads expected to increase by 2022. Mobile marketing companies have progressively used phone apps as just a marketplace

Designs of APP Advertising

1. Content integrated method mostly for Application development companies' prerequisite a way to repatriate implantable advertisements. APP integrates content marketing and gaming to effortlessly mix customer involvement to progress advertisement successes. With any of these free download applications, designers benefit from in app acquisitions and subscriptions.

2. In most ad applications, promotional template implantation is a common marketing method. Customers jump to the given page via online ads, customer announcements, as well as in-screen advertising and show contextual ads when consumers click. This template is more natural and easily draws users' interest.

3. Client engagement feature refers for domain transplant and product APP. For users to access, the business releases its very own app to the APP store, and customers can understand better the information. This Software provides great comfort

to consumer as a necessary tool. Customer comparison mode allows consumers to have a much more intense experience. So, consumers can know the product, enhance the company's brand image, and capture the user heart.

4. Integrated shopping portal style is the conventional Online business offering services in the mobile phone app, which is easy for consumers to search product data whenever, wherever, for to buy and order monitoring. This system has endorsed the conversion of conventional e-commerce enterprises from shopping to mobile web channels, which would be a required way of using mobile APPs for immersive digital and physical growth, such as Amazon, eBay, etc. The above said few trends for more common advertising strategies, for the specifics while not being listed too much, but hope will help you get a basic knowledge of APP advertising and go further in advertising on the market.

In-Game Mobile Marketing

Mobile gaming has three main patterns: animated real-time 3D games, multi-player games, as well as social media games. It indicates a step toward more nuanced, advanced, comfortable game play. In a different view, there are so-called casual games. Games are quite easy as well as simple to play. Many mobile games nowadays are informal games, so it likely stays that way for rather a while to derive.

Brands offer marketing advertisements in mobile games and promote the whole game to boost customer interest. It is recognized as the mobile advertisement gaming or advertisement funded virtual game.

In mobile advertising in-game, promoters pay to display their title or goods in mobile games. Racing game can be conducted in actual virtual vehicles. In the efforts to incorporate ads naturally into mobile games the marketers must be imaginative and dominant.

Expenditure in mobile marketing techniques especially in ad gaming is slightly cheaper than the Ad designed for a mobile app. A good tactic can create the product branding and it can produce significant income. Advertisement game makes users to recall the product and brand in a better way. This remembering improves viral marketing so people tend to suggest it to friends and relatives, and share it via social media.

One type of phone game advertisements allows people to play. A modern and successful form of advertising helps users to check the product before downloading it. Such type of advertising may also generate users publicity like casual gamers. These ads blur the game-to-advertising lines and to provide teams with a deeper experience that enables them to devote their valuable time communicating with advertisements.

That is not only fascinating; it also gives many incentives for advertisers. such digital ads can generate more efficient conversion rates because they are social and have higher processing velocities than general advertisements. Players may also give a greater value proposition. They pre-measure product performance to provide further in-depth information. This type of activity can improve user adhesion more effectively than advertisements networks such as tales and video.

Mobile Advertising and Location-Based Services

Many mobile phone networks provide location-based services (LBS) as a way of sending personalized advertisements and other data to mobile phone users based on their individual position. The cellular service supplier receives the destination from either a GPS chip constructed into the mobile, and using radio location depending on the signal strength of the nearest cell towers (for GPS-free phones).

Many Location Based services operate without GPS tracking, instead sharing data between same level gadgets or phones.

There have been different methods for businesses to use a device's position.

1. ***Shop localizers:*** Use place-based data, retail customers easily find the closest specific store.

2. ***Location-based Advertising:*** Organizations may distribute ads to people in the same place. Site-based services send ads to potential clients of an area who can actually take intervention on data.

3. ***Voyage data:*** Site-based services could provide real mobile time data like traffic situation or weather, and users can create the schedule.

4. ***Services on the road:*** For rapid road accidents, the travel insurance firm can make an app to monitor the actual-time location of the client without mapping.

Ring Less Voicemail

Wireless technology has made it easy to send a voice message on a mobile even without ringing. VoAPP developed the software as a debt collection system in relation to living users. The Federal Communications Commission (FCC) found the software complies with all legislation. Cost Per Lead (CPL) built on current technology that allows a fully automated system, like replacing live employees with non-recorded messages.

Conclusion

Mobile advertisement is becoming increasingly popular. Few mobile advertisements, which is being sent without the customer's necessary permission generating violations of privacy. It must be acknowledged that regardless of how marketing campaigns are crafted and how many additional options they have, if users do not believe that their privacy will be covered, this will impede their broad distribution. But when the communications come from a place in which the client is participating in a friendship/rewards program, confidentiality is not infringed and even disruptions may create gratitude.

The legal issue of privacy was even more prevalent as cellular data services appeared. Number of significant new issues arose primarily because devices were closely social. There are four concerns that are always recognized with customers: phone spam, proof of identity, destination as well as mobile security. The overall mobile phone app activity could be monitored in a security-preserving manner.

Chapter – 9

SEARCH ENGINE MARKETING (SEM)

Introduction

Search engine marketing, or SEM, was designed to enhance website exposure in search engine outcome (SERPs) pages. Search engines offer additional sponsored outcomes as well as organic (non-sponsored) outcomes grounded on a website search. Browsers often use graphics to distinguish sponsored content from natural results. Search engine optimization (CEO) covers the activities of an advertising company to get a domain page more popular with relevant keyword. The main reason underneath SEM's increasing popularity was Google. Several businesses had their own PPC and Analytics software. Hence, Google made this term popular. Google Ad words helped marketers use and build ads. Then, they found the device was doing a fair job, paying just for somebody's click on the ad, which recorded as the cost-per-click in which a cent was paid. It prompted marketers to control the advertisement by the number of likes and were pleased that advertisements could be monitored.

1. *Search Engine Optimization (SEO):* Search engine optimization, or SEO, tries to enhance search results ratings in SERPs by expanding the significance of website content in order of search words. Search engines upgrade their computer programs frequently to penalize low quality webpages trying to play their rankings, attempting to do optimization a specific target of marketers. Most sites offer SEO.

2. *Sponsored scanning*: Supported search (also called supported references, search ads, or paid search) requires marketers to be used in the funded search engine results. Google advertisements are often offered by real-time auctions, whereby marketers bid keywords. Besides attempting to set a floor price per key word, tenders can include time, vocabulary, geological, and other limitations. Search engines initially sold ads for top bids. Contemporary search engines classify funded listings depending on bid price mixture, anticipated scroll-through rate, key word relevance and site performance.

3. *Online marketing*: Online marketing is selling via social media platforms. Many businesses promote their goods through regular updates and special offers via their profiles. This procedure includes videos, immersive questionnaires and link backs. Normally, these kinds of advertisements are seen on twitter, Pinterest, Twitter, and Snapchat.

4. *Mobile marketing*: Mobile marketing is supplied via mobile devices like smartphones, handsets or personal computers. Online advertising may consist of variable or interactive content display advertisements, SMS (Short Message Service) or MMS (Multimedia Messaging Service) advertisements, mobile search advertisements, advertisements on mobile websites or advertisements on mobile apps or games.

Mobile advertising rises rapidly for several reasons. There are mobile apps in the market, networking rates have increased, display sizes have progressed. Digital advertisers have become more and more knowledgeable in adding advertisements, and users are constantly utilizing phones and tablets. The Digital Advertising Bureau expects steady growth of mobile ads by site-based advertising as well as other technical capabilities that are not accessible or applicable on desktop computers. So that, online advertising income compensated for a huge rise over the past years.

5. Email advertisements: Email marketing is an advertisement duplication consisting of a whole online or an email message. Email advertising may be spontaneous, by which circumstance the transmitter may provide the receiver with an ability to opt for future messages, or with a receiver's prior approval. Companies can request for the Email ID and can actually send product or sales notifications.

6. Chat advertisement: Chat ads, unlike fixed communication, applies to real-time updates delivered to consumers with certain pages. This is achieved using web chat technology and monitoring apps built for certain pages, with running personnel behind the page frequently losing ads on people browsing around the internet. This is basically a form of email marketing, but unique due to its window of time.

7. Classified online marketing: Digital classified ads are inbound marketing in a numerical list of common products or services. Types provide online job boards, online real estate listings, vehicle classifieds, and online business pages and sale-based listings.

8. The adware: Adware is technology which automatically exhibits ads on a user's device once configured. Ads can display in the code itself, embedded in user-visited webpages, or in pop-ups or pop-under. Adware installing without customer consent is malicious and immoral.

9. Affiliate Marketing: Affiliate advertising happens whenever marketers combine third parties to build prospective customers. Third-party affiliates receive money depending on their promotional sales. Affiliate marketers produce congestion to affiliate network deals, and when visitors start taking the required action, the affiliate receives a payment. Such required activities could be an email post, a phone call, a simple online form or perhaps an online request.

10. Content Marketing: Content marketing would be any advertisement including developing or distributing information or releasing digital to attract or keep customers. This data could be provided in a variety of media such as blog sites, news, audio, research papers, e-books, data visuals, studies, manuals, etc.

Almost all advertising requires any type of published materials. There will be many types of advertising where the tag is more helpful to distinguish marketing category. Furthermore, it seems that it simply provides material and they are marketing information in a better form than print media, Television, movie, email, or Internet media.

11. Online Marketing system: Digital marketing framework is an incorporated internet-based platform that integrates the advantages of a company database, web search engine, SEO tool, Client relationship Management (CRM) and Web Content System. Amazon and eBay are being used as Internet marketing as well as logistical support platforms. Retailing also has been used on Twitter, Facebook, YouTube as well as other social networks.

Except for TV marketing where Nielsen TV Ratings can be used to view indicators; internet marketers have no independent group to confirm watching claims being made by large online systems.

12. Remuneration methods: Marketers and publishing houses use a variety of payment measurement techniques. In 2018, marketers measured 42 percent of online ad purchases on a price-per-print basis, 50 percent on product experience, and 8 percent on perception or quality combinations.

13. CPM (cost/mille): Price per mille, also referred to CPM, implies companies pay prospective customers for thousands shows of their advertisement (mille is really the Latin term for thousand). In the internet framework, ad screens are known as "impressions". Explanations of "assumption" differ between many advertisers, and maybe some perceptions may not be indicted as they do not offer a new consumer visibility. Marketers could use systems like Internet bugs to confirm if an experience is really delivered. Publishing companies use a variety of methods to boost page views, like splitting material across multiple pages, repurposing material, use dramatic titles, or writing tabloid, etc.

CPM marketing is vulnerable to "assumption fraud," and marketers who wish to get customers to the web pages might not find a decent firewall for the outcomes they need.

1. CPC *(cost/click)*: CPC (Cost Per Click) or PPC (Pay per click) implies companies pay whenever a user enters to their advertisement. CPC marketing works well because marketers need traffic to the pages, but this is a less accurate indicator of marketers who want brand recognition. Since the first launch, CPC's share of the market has risen steadily, surpassing CPM to control two-thirds of all online ad payout systems.

Like views, all interactions are not beneficial for marketers. Gold Spot Media has reported that around 45 percent of fixed digital banner advertising clicks were unintended, resulting in diverted users quitting a new site instantly.

2. CPE *(cost/engagement)*: Cost per engagement is intended to monitor not only an ad facility loaded onto the site but also the audience simply have seen or cooperated paths with the advertisement.

3. CPV *(cost/view)*: Cost per vision of video promotion. Google as well as Tube Mogul have supported this structured CPV definition to the IAB's (Innovative Advertisement Bureau) Digital Video Panel, attracting significant public and company support. CPV is the key metric used by Google's Ad Words program for YouTube Advertisements.

4. CPI *(cost/install)*: CPI remuneration technique is particular to phone advertising. In CPI campaigns, products are indicted a specified bid percentage only after installing the application.

5. *Value attribution*: In advertising, "attribution" is the calculation of the efficacy of specific ads in the customer's final buying decision. Numerous ad views can guide to a "click" or other intervention. A single move may lead to multiple advertisements zone where sellers receive income.

6. *Performance-based rewards:* CPA (Cost Per Action or Cost Per Acquisition) or PPP (Pay Performance) marketing implies the advertising company ends up paying the number of users performing a required behavior, like achieving a transaction or finalizing an application form. Quality-based rewards can also include profit sharing, in which the advertising company receives a portion of the advertising gain. Quality-based pay changes the threat of ineffective publishers' advertisements.

7. *Fixed Cost:* Fixed cost remuneration implies marketers pay a fixed price for the distribution of advertisement in online, typically over a set period of time, regardless of the ad's traction or user reaction. Another instance is CPD (cost per day) whereby marketers pay a monthly sum to post an ad for the day, regardless of views or views.

8. *Online-advertising costs:* Similar with offline advertising, small digital communication rates lower the cost of viewing online advertising. Digital advertising, especially social networking, offers small cost for marketers to interact with large international audiences. Internet advertising yields stronger than most other media.

9. *Measurability:* Internet marketers can collect information on the efficacy of their advertisements, like the volume of the customer base or real audience reaction, how well a visitor attained their advertising, whether all the advertising campaign culminated in a sale, whether an image actually packed in a passenger's view. It supports advertisers to develop their advertising operations for all the time.

10. *Formatting:* Marketers have many ways to introduce their advertisement, including that of the ability to communicate pictures, audio, video, and references. Unlike some other online ads, online advertising may be immersive. Many advertisings, for instance, let clients insert questions and track the advertisement company on social networks. Online advertising can even include games.

11. Targeting: Marketers may suggest advertisers the ability to achieve customized target market and specific markets. Digital advertising can use geo-targeting to show specific advertising for consumer geographically. Marketers may tailor that ad to a specific user based on past display settings. Marketers may also track how well a visitor is seeing a particular website to minimize undesired repetitive exposures and to provide sufficient gaps around exposures.

12. Coverage: Digital advertising can potentially reach each global market, and off-line advertising affects sales.

13. Rapidity: When ad development is complete, advertising online could be launched instantly. Online advertising distribution cannot be related to the editor's release schedule. Digital marketers can also change and delete ad copies quicker than the offline equivalents.

Technological Variations

1. Heterogeneous customers: Since consumers use different platforms, browsers and computer components, such as phones and tablets and different user sizes, online advertising can look different to users than the marketers expected, or advertising may not show correctly. Multimedia advertisements pose larger performance issues, as some programmers might use competing programs for display advertisements. In addition, marketers may experience legal issues if legally obligatory data does not show to users, even though that inability is due to technical diversity.

2. Blocking: Ad blocking, or ad screening, ensures advertisements do not show to the consumer because the client utilizes ad scanning software. Most sites avoid pop-up ads by definition. Certain software programs and app add-on might also restrict the downloading of advertisements, or disable ad behavioral features on a website. Roughly 9 percent of all web page views originate from devices with enabled ad-blocking software, and some websites have 40 percent+ of their users use ad-blockers.

3. *Anti-targeting innovation:* Many browsers provide privacy settings where consumers can mask their data from advertisers and marketers. Marketers cannot use cookies to deliver targeted advertisements to private users. Many big developers have integrated Do Not Track choices into their tab heads, but still only the honor system enforces the rules.

4. *Privacy considerations:* Collecting sensitive information by publishing companies and content providers expressed consumer concern about their confidentiality. Sixty percent of Users would be using Do Not Trace software to restrict any information gathering if given a chance. According to Gallup, about half of all Google and Facebook customers were worried with their security using Google and Facebook.

5. *Advertisers credibility:* Scammers may take full advantage of the complexities of customers checking a digital identity of a person. Customers pose ransom ware threats when engaging with digital advertising. For instance, in August 2014, Yahoo's advertising network allegedly had instances of Crypto locker ransom ware infection.

6. *Spam:* The low price of Online advertising spreading directly relates to spam, particularly by huge-scale hackers. Various attempts have been made to fight spam, from black lists to regulatory-required branding to Internet blockers, but most of these initiatives have negative unintended consequences, such as misunderstood filtering.

7. *Ordinance:* Generally, Customer laws apply equally to offline and online operations. Nonetheless, there are concerns about the rules of authority extend and which government agencies have over trans-border operation.

Unlike online marketing, market actors made numerous attempts to self-regulate or establish company standards and guidelines. Key concepts of both agreements provide user regulation over data transmission to private entities, security, and agreement to obtain such financial and health data.

8. Privacy, data gathering: Privacy regulations may involve super user privileges before an ad company that can track or interact with the user. Nonetheless, securing verbal consent can be difficult and costly. Also, market members favor other regulatory systems.

Different countries took different solutions regarding commercial privacy concerns. The US has specific limits on electronic baby monitoring in the Children's Online Privacy Protection Act (COPPA). The authorities have recently expanded its COPPA definition to include allowing ad networks to seek parental permission before actively monitoring children. Then Consumer financial protection bureau commonly promotes self-regulation in the industry, while it has progressively undertaken legal actions regarding online privacy and safety.

By comparison, the EU's "Privacy and Electronic Communications Directive" restricts the ability of Web pages to use consumer information more extensively. EU restrictions limit targeting by internet advertisers; researchers calculated digital advertising efficacy in Europe reduces by about 65 percent on average relative to the rest of the globe.

Conclusion

Many customers reserve from online intellectual observing. By monitoring internet activity of users, marketers can comprehend consumers well. Marketers sometimes use innovation, like Web bugs and reacting cookies, to optimize their tracking ability. As per a study conducted by Harris Interactive, about half of online users used to have a negative image of digital ads, and 40 percent believed that marketers have exchanged their private information despite their permission. Customers can be particularly disturbed by targeted marketers predicated on sensitive data, such as economic or body habitus. In fact, many marketers bind the address of client phones to their population accounts' so that, they can be refocused even though the consumer removes their cookie or search history.

Chapter - 10

PAY-PER-CLICK (PPC)

Pay-per-click (PPC), also regarded as cost per click (CPC), is an online advertising system used only to direct people to web sites where an ad company pays publishing company while the advertisement is clicked.

Pay-per-click is usually associated to search engines like Google Ads and Bing Ads, etc. Using search engines, marketers suggest the key phrases important to the target audience. Conversely, social bookmarking sites usually charge a fixed price per tap instead of a bidding process. PPC "display" ads, also recognized as "banner" ads, are displayed on related posts Web pages which have agreed to demonstrate ads and are usually not pay-per-click advertisements. Social media sites like Facebook and Twitter have already embraced pay-per-click as the marketing designs.

Websites can deliver PPC advertising. Sites that use PPC ads can exhibit advertisements whenever a search query matches the keyword list of an advertising company added in different ad groups, or if a content page exhibits quality content. These ads are termed sponsored links or endorsed advertisements and seem to adjacent to, up or down organic outcomes on web browser outcomes pages or wherever a software developer chooses a material site. The PPC advertising model is open for abuse by selecting fraud while Google and many others have introduced automated processes to prevent abuse by rivals and dishonest web designers.

Purpose

Pay-per-click, together with price per admiration and price per request, is used to measure online marketing's costs-effectiveness and competitiveness. Pay-per-click (PPC) has a benefit over price per experience by conveying information of how an effective ad is. Clicks are a way of measuring attention and support. If the primary purpose of an ad is to produce a click, or more precisely lead movement to a location, the chosen measure is PPC. When a certain percentage of Web views are reached, the advertisements' consistency and positioning can affect clicking through frequency and the subsequent PPC.

Cost-Per-Click (CPC)

The Unit of CPC is computed through the division of advertising costs by an number of clicks in which an advertisement generates. The simple formula seems to be: Cost-per-click)($ = Marketing cost ($)/ Ads clicked (#). There are two main frameworks of PPC: plain-rate and based on bid. For both cases, the ad company should recognize a provided source's possible click value. That value depends on the kind of person the advertising company receives as a visitor to its site, as well as what the advertising company will benefit from that visit, typically income both long term and short term. As with all types of marketing, major factors which often fit into PPC strategies have included the focus on the customer.

Flat-Rate PPC

The ad company and publishing company concur on a fixed sum for each click in the flat-rate system. In several instances, the author does have a rate card showing PPC for various areas of the site or system. Such different quantities are sometimes linked to material on websites, with material that typically draws more valued visitors lead to higher PPC than material that attract less valued visits. In several situations, though, marketers may negotiate for better prices, particularly when agreeing to the long-period or strong-value contracts.

The flat-rate method is popular with related to retail systems, which usually release rating cards. Such prices can sometimes be small, though; the marketers may charge more for better exposure. Typically, these pages are conveniently tightly controlled into goods and service classes, enabling marketers to aim extremely. In several instances, such sites' entire structure of content is PPC.

Bid-Based PPC

The advertising company enters to an agreement allowing them to negotiate with other marketers in a public auction sponsored by a publisher or, more generally, an advertising company. The advertising company tells the hosts of the maximum they are prepared to pay for a specific ad spot, typically utilizing online resources. The sale is programed every time a client activates the advertisement.

Once the advertising spot is a part of Google Search Results page (SERP), the automated sale occurs when a Web search happens. All keywords bids targeting the searcher's geo-location, and the day and date of the search, then this is measured and the result is decided. For cases where several ad positions are popular on SERPs, there may be multiple candidates whose locations on the list are determined by the sum each offer thy have. Bid and Value Rating were used to rate each entrepreneur's advertisement. The advertisement with both the largest ad grade appears first. Google and Bing's primary three game styles are Broad, Exact, and Phrase match. Google often provides the Broad Match Modifier form which varies from wide match, as the keyword should contain the real word words in any sequence and does not include applicable terms variants.

In contrast to commercial spots on SERPs, the big advertising platforms permit situational advertisements to be put on third-party sites which they have collaborated with. Such sites sign up for site host advertising.

In exchange, they take a percentage of the advertising revenue that the network produces, between 50 percent to over 80 percent of marketers' gross income. Such sites are sometimes referred to as a web channel and the advertisements on them equally as contextual ads even though the ad spot are connected to keyword depending on the background of the website they are located on. Overall, ads on material networks have a lower scroll-through rate (CTR) as well as exchange rate (CR) than ads on SERPs and are therefore less appreciated. Network material can include internet sites, bulletins, and emails.

Conclusion

Sponsors pay for each tap they get, with both the actual sum rewarded based on the quantity of bid. It is normal practice between many auction presenters to pay a buyer slightly than the next bidder or the real bid percentage, which would be even smaller. This eliminates circumstances in which bidders continuously change their bids under very small quantities and see if they can also win the sale while going to pay less per button.

Computerized bid network topologies can be implemented to optimize performance and size. The ad company uses these tools directly, although they are most widely used by ad agencies delivering PPC bid control as a product. Such systems allow on-scale bid control, with millions or even billions of PPC bids managed by an automated process. The system usually lays each offer premised on the target set for everything, such as maximizing profit, maximizing traffic, even getting the much directed consumer at break, etc. Generally, the structure is tied in to the advertising site and fed each click's outcomes, allowing this to set bids. The efficacy of these structures is directly linked to the volume and quality of the data with whom they have to work. Small traffic ads can result in a shortages of data issue that makes several bid admin tools useless at the worst, or ineffective at the greatest.

Chapter - 11

SOCIAL MEDIA MARKETING

Introduction

Presently, Social Media Marketing is the using of online channels and sites to advertise products or service. While the concepts e-marketing and electronic marketing also prevail in higher education, social marketing becomes more prominent for both professionals and scientists. Many social media sites have constructed-in analytics tools enabling businesses to track advertising campaign advancement, achievement, and engagement. By social media, corporations target a variety of investors, comprising current and prospective clients, actual and potential staff, reporters, writers, and the public in general. On a tactical level, social marketing involves maintaining an advertising campaign, governance, defining context and establishing the ideal social media "community" or "voice" of a company. Using online marketing, companies may also enable users and Web browsers to post customer generated content.

Social Networking Websites

Social media sites permit people, companies, and other agencies to communicate and construct online relationships as well as digital neighborhoods. Once businesses enter these media networks, customers may communicate directly. The engagement could be more private to consumers than conventional advertising and marketing approaches. Social media platforms function as mouth-words and more specifically, e-word mouth. The potential of the Web to touch billions worldwide has provided strong voice and far-reaching digital social media. The capacity to immediately change shopping habits, service or product procurement and operation to an increasing number of customers is characterized as a system of impact. Sites and forums encourage supporters to "retweet" or "update" posts about a brand being advertised that appears very regularly on certain social networking sites. Restating the signal enables user to contacts, see message and approaching more people. Even though the safety information is being placed there and replicated, the product and company gets more publicity.

Web pages of social media are founded on virtual groups that allow consumers online to convey their requirements, needs and principles. Social marketing binds these customers and viewers with corporations that have the very same interests, desires and principles. Using social media, businesses can reach specific followers. This social interaction may instill commitment in supporters and prospective customers. Companies can also hit a very small target market by simply following on these pages. Social media sites have included data on what goods and services potential customers might be involved in. Using new linguistic analysis systems, marketers can pinpoint purchasing messages such as people-shared material and questions that asked via internet. Knowing purchasing signs can help retailers to identify specific customers, and advertisers to execute micro-target initiatives.

Mobile Phones

Over three billion individuals are active on social media. Throughout the years, the Web has attracted ever more subscribers, around 738 million people in 2012 to 3.2 billion in 2020. About 81 percent of the actual U.S. population has some kind of social media profile they often interact in. Mobile phones is useful for digital marketing due to their internet browsing features allowing people to access social network sites instantly. Mobile phones changed the path to purchase and by allowing consumers to easily obtain real-time retail prices and customer information. We also enabled businesses to keep reminding and inform their supporters. Several businesses are now placing Quick Response (QR) protocols together with products to obtain the website or internet services with their smartphones. Manufacturers use Smartphone apps to promote customer engagement by connecting the code to company pages, ads, information, and other smartphone content. However, in the mobile ad industry, real-time bid use has been strong and growing owing to its importance for on-the-go Internet browsing.

Passive Approach for Social Networks

Social networking can be a valuable market data tool and a means to gain customer views. Blogs, online groups, and platforms are sites where people exchange product, brand, commodity, and service feedback and suggestions. Companies are able to transform and evaluate the consumer tones and responses produced in social networks for advertising purposes, in this sense social networking is a relatively affordable source of industry intelligence that advertisers and executives could use to monitor and react to customer-identified issues and identify business opportunities. For example, the Internet erupted with iPhone 6 "bend test" videos and pictures showing the prestigious phone can be clamped by side pressure. These so-called "bend door" uproar led to confusion between people waiting weeks to release the iPhone's new version. Nevertheless, Apple immediately released a statement that the situation was exceedingly rare and the company took numerous steps to make the case of the smartphone safer and stable. While normal market research methodology such as market survey, opinion polls, and data mining that are time-consuming and expensive and require weeks or months to study, advertisers can use social media to collect online and real-time human behavior insights and opinions on a company's brand or goods.

Active Approach for Social Networks

Social networks should be used not just as public affairs and direct mail tools and also as communications channels trying to target quite specific audiences with influences and social media personality traits and as an efficient consumer commitment tools. Technologies predating social networking, like broadcast television and magazines, can provide a relatively target audience for advertisers. Social media platforms, though, can reach niche markets more specifically. Through digital tools like Google AdSense, marketers may tailor promotion ads to particular demographics like people interested in the social empowerment, political engagement related to a particular political group, or computer gaming. Google AdSense does so by finding key words in internet comments and replies from social network users. It would also be difficult for a Television station or newspaper and provide targeted advertisements.

Social networks are often considered a great weapon to avoid costly market research. They are considered to provide a short, quick and easy way of reaching a market through a well-known person. For instance, a sportsman who gets supported by a home goods firm also brings their support base to billions of consumers who are interested in what they do or how they are playing, now they want to be aspect of this sportsman through their approval of the firm. Until one time customers would visit retailers to see their goods featuring famous celebrities, but you could still see a famous athlete like Cristiano Ronaldo, the new online clothing with a key press. He delivers directly via his Snapchat, Facebook, and Online accounts.

Interaction on Social Media

Social network involvement means consumers and stakeholders are participants, not passive spectators. For instance, consumer protection groups or organizations who are opposing businesses using social networks in a company or sociocultural context enables all customers and citizens to convey and discuss an opinion on the goods, facilities, practices or actions of a corporation. A contributing consumer, non-consumer, or person engaging online via social networks is part of a marketing team and they may read this positively or negatively on the product or services. Engaging customers, future users, and people digitally is important to for the effective digital marketing. With the emergence of digital marketing, consumer engagement in goods and services is becoming increasingly relevant. It can finally be converted into purchasing actions, and voting patterns in a political environment. New Internet advertising principles of interaction and retention arose to create consumer interest and brand image.

Social networking participation in marketing plan is split into two sections. First, constructive, that means periodic posting of additional content in Internet. Through Online images, online videos, email, and messages one could see this. It has also been expressed by posting content and other data via weblinks. The second section is proactive interactions with people on social media reacting by responding and talking to all those who hit the social media accounts. Traditional media like TV news programs are restricted to one-way customer contact or "push and tell" in which only basic information was provided to viewers with little to minimal feedback loops. Traditional media like physical papers require people to send the writer a message. It is a fairly slow procedure, however, as the editorial staff will evaluate the letter to determine if it is suitable for publishing. Social networking, at the other hand, is participatory and free; users can immediately express their opinions on brands and products. Traditional media showed the marketing expert power of statement, while social networking shifts equalize to the customer or citizen.

Local Businesses Marketing by Social Media

Small companies use social media sites as a marketing tool. Companies can follow international uses of person social networks and promote special offers and deals. These may be exclusive to the "have a free meal with such a message". This form of statement promotes other local people to follow on-site company to get the licensing deal. The company gets seen by it and markets itself.

Small business owners also utilize social media platforms to build the independent consumer research for new products. By promoting their consumers to provide input on new product ideas, companies can gain additional insights into whether or not a brand can be approved by their target audience for full operation. Additionally, clients may feel the business has involved them throughout the non-creation process. The process where the company uses feedback from customers to develop or alter a products or services that fills a target market need. These reviews can take different forms, like surveys, competitions, interviews, etc.

Social media sites like Facebook do provide resources for small companies to seek applicants to fill vacant positions. Websites like Yelp also help businesses develop an image through product recognition. Beneficial product peer reviews potentially influence new opportunities to purchase goods more than political propaganda.

Twitter

Twitter helps companies to market their products in simple messages recognized as tweets restricted to 140 characters introduced on house timelines. Tweets may include text, hashtag, picture, video, animated GIF, and references to the brand site as well as other social media accounts, etc. Companies also use Twitter for customer service. Many companies are offering assistance 24/7 and response, and consequently increasing customer loyalty and recognition.

Facebook

Facebook pages are wider than Twitter feeds. They enable a brand provide videos, pictures, larger descriptions, and case studies where supporters can post for everyone to see on product descriptions. Facebook will link directly to the Twitter page of the company and submit activity notifications. Since 2015, 93 percent of advertisers used Facebook to promote their product. A 2011 report credited 84 percent of "interaction" and taps, or likes to link back to Facebook ads. By 2014,

Facebook limited material from company and product pages. Changes in Facebook technology have lowered viewers to un-paying business pages.

LinkedIn

LinkedIn, a specialized company-related social network, helps companies to develop business profiles and connect with others. Using plugins, participants can advertise their different social media practices on their Facebook profile page, such as Twitter stream and blog posts on their product pages. LinkedIn helps its participants to create market managers and business associates. Representatives can use Facebook-like "Company Pages" to develop an area where businesses can advertise their products as well as services and communicate with their clients. Because spam mails are sent to job seekers, top companies chose to just use LinkedIn to hire employees rather than using a specific job gateway. Businesses also expressed a choice for the volume of information which can be collected from a LinkedIn profile rather than one of a restricted email.

WhatsApp

Jan Koum with Brian Acton formed WhatsApp. WhatsApp amalgamated Facebook in 2014, but operates as a distinct app to construct a worldwide fast and reliable messaging app. WhatsApp emerged as an addition to SMS. WhatsApp now promotes transmitting a range of sources such as text, pictures, videos, records, destination, and voice calls. WhatsApp messages and communications are encrypted with end-to-end authentication, ensuring no third party can read or listen to them, except WhatsApp. WhatsApp does have a 1billion client base in over 180 nations. It used to send single product marketing emails. It has several benefits over SMS, including tracking how Messenger Broadcast executes using WhatsApp's blue tick tool. It enables sending messages to clients. WhatsApp often uses the broadcast option of sending a sequence of bulk texts to directed customers. Companies have started to use primarily because this is a price-effective marketing tool and easy to convey a message. Today, WhatsApp forbids companies from placing ads in the app.

Instagram

Instagram reported over 300 million subscribers in May 2014. Instagram's usage rate is more when compared to other social networking sites. As per Scott Galloway, L2 founding member and advertising professor at New York University's Stern Business school, studies calculate that 93 percent of high-end brands are active on Social media and included in their advertising mix. When it relates to products and enterprises, Instagram aims to help businesses meet their specific markets by captivating images in a warm, immersive atmosphere. Instagram also provides a framework for users and businesses to interact publicly and specifically, rendering it an ideal choice for businesses to link with their current and prospective consumers.

Most companies use this mobile phone app to improve their marketing plan. Instagram could be used to generate the power needed to secure market segment awareness that is involved in product offerings and services. As Apple as well as android support Instagram, smartphone users are allowed to access it. It can also be reached by both the Internet. The marketing companies see it as a prospective model to broaden their web stores' exposure, particularly younger target demographic. In addition, marketers are also using social networks for conventional Online advertising, but also allow users to focus on a certain brand. It usually provides an opportunity for brand awareness. Often, advertisers use the site to push online shopping and encourage people to pick up and share photos of their favorite brands.

Snapchat

Snapchat is indeed a common implementation which was produced in 2011 by three graduates: Evan Spiegel, Bobby Murphy, and Reggie

Brown – at Stanford. The application had first been created to enable users send back the messages and forward and to show pictures which are only accessible from 1–10 seconds when they are no longer obtainable. The app was also an immediate hit with social networking members, or currently up to 158 million individuals use snapchat every day. Snapchat consumers are also calculated to close the implementation about 18 times a day, meaning users are on the app for around 25–30 minutes per day.

YouTube

YouTube is yet another common option where commercials are designed to suit target groups. Style of language used during advertisements and concepts used to make sales represent the taste and style of the viewer. Advertisements on this channel are typically aligned with the quality of the submitted video and it is another benefit YouTube gives to marketers. Most advertisements include such clips as the material is appropriate. Advertising opportunity like endorsing content is also available on YouTube, for instance, a customer who is looking for just a Video on YouTube about training dogs can be met with a supported video from either a dog toy manufacturer in result along with much other content. YouTube also helps advertisers to make money via its freelancer Program.

Social Bookmarking Sites

Web sites like Delicious, Digg, Slashdot, Diigo, StumbleUpon, and Reddit are famous social bookmarking sites utilized in online place. In media networking sites, each one of these pages is devoted to storing, supervising and coordinating references to other sites that consumers consider good value. This system is "crowded," requiring participants of professional social networking sites to filter and prioritize connections by importance and broad classification. The smallest site may be in a burst crowd, a massive increase in interest throughout the goal website given the large user base of these sites. Including client-generated advertising, these platforms often deliver advertising inside user groups and classes.

Since advertisements can be positioned in specified populations with a specific target market and preferences, they have much higher potential for demand creation than ads merely chosen by cookie and browsing history. In contrast, most of these platforms have also introduced reforms to make advertising more user relevant by encouraging users to vote on which sites they often view. The opportunity to channel large Internet volume of traffic and reach small, appropriate users allows social bookmarking sites a valuable asset to social networking marketers.

Blogs

Platforms such as LinkedIn build a networking environment between businesses and consumers. Organizations who understand any need for data, creativity and transparency use blogs to make their work famous and distinctive and eventually for to reaching out to customers privately-owned social networks. Statistics show that viewers regard news or blogger reporting as more objective and reliable than advertisements that are not considered free or autonomous. Blogs enable a brand or organization provides longer service or product reviews, may include reports, and may connect to other social media network and blog sites. Blogs could be modified regularly, and are marketing tactics to keep fans, as well as to attract fans and viewers who could then be guided to social media sites. Social media platforms can allow company to meet other corporate customers using the web. To encourage firms to assess their status in the business world, places encourage workers to position their organization reviews. Many companies refuse to integrate social media sites into their traditional advertising system. General business standard applies when communicating online. To retain an edge in a business-customer partnership, companies must be mindful of four key assets that customers hold: data, interaction, group, and power to control.

Tumblr

Blogging platform Tumblr initially introduced ad services in 2012. Instead of focusing on simplistic advertisements, Tumblr allows marketers to build a Tumblr blog so that blog posts can be displayed on the platform. In an year, multiple native ad forms were developed on the mobile platforms and much more than 100 Tumblr brands advertised with a 500 aggregate sponsored content.

Advertisement Framework

Mobile updates sponsoring: Advertising can be displayed on the consumer page whenever the individual is on mobile devices such as phones and laptops, enabling them to like, reblog and retweet the post.

Blog post Sponsoring: The Web's biggest in-stream ad device that captures users' interest while accessing their Home page from their laptop or desktop. This also allows audiences to comment, reblog, and post.

Radar sponsoring: Radar selects outstanding content from those in the entire Tumblr community on their intellectual and creative content. This is put on the right side beside the Dash board, usually receiving 120 million average interactions. Sponsored radar helps marketers to position their comments there to gain new fans, reblogs, and views.

Spotlight sponsoring: Spotlight is indeed a list of many popular blogs in a group, as well as a location which people can find new websites to follow. Advertisers must choose one from under fifty groups that always have the blog listed online. Such blogs can have more ability to follow: photos, picture collections, video clips, video, voice, and textual content. To distinguish the sponsored posts from normal user comments, the sponsored posts get a dollar sign on the bottom.

Online Marketing Methods

Online marketing entails using social media, customer's online brand-related activities (COBRA) and Electronic word of mouth (eWOM) to communicate online effectively. Social media like Twitter and Facebook notify marketers related to their clients' tastes and preferences. This strategy is important as it offers to companies with an audience. Companies provide access to the information specific to the user's interests of social networks; then promote appropriately. Things like uploading a photo of your "new Converse shoes" on Facebook. It is COBRA's illustration. Electronic reviews and ratings are the useful ways to get a brand advertised by "customer-to-consumer" experiences. An illustration of eWOM is a digital hotel rating; the hospitality provider could have two potential outcomes depending on their performance. An excellent service would lead in a glowing review which would offer the hotel more business.

Social networking site is yet another medium that company and marketers will seek to influence. Unlike non-Internet marketing, like Television advertising and advertisements on print media, where the marketing company manage all facets of the advertisement, in social networks. Consumers are free to share comments under a firm's Internet ad or blog message on their brand. Industries are constantly utilizing their social media strategy as part with a traditional advertising campaign including journals, newsletters, radio ads, television ads. consumers often use platforms concurrently in the 2010s (e.g.: Web browsing on a laptop while viewing a streaming TV show), promotional material needs to be more consistent in all outlets, whether conventional or digital media. Scholars Speak about, how much exposure the companies can pay to the social media. It is more about finding the balance in blogging, and not over submitting. There need to provide more importance to social networking sites, because consumers use alerts to obtain brand awareness.

Scheduled material starts with the innovative/marketing department creating their proposals, after finishing their thoughts they submit for acceptance and sanction. There are two specific forms to do this. Primarily, the company accepts the project one after the other, publisher, and product, accompanied by the team of lawyers. Industries can vary in size and market philosophy. The second would be where growing business is provided 24 hours to register or reject. When no actions are taken within 24 hours, the initial plan is implemented. Planned material is sometimes visible to consumers, mis-original or lacking anticipation, but is also a better option to prevent unwanted public backlash. All paths; for scheduled material are time-consuming like in the above authorization requires 72 hours for the very first path. Even though the second path can be slightly shorter, it also brings more uncertainty in the human resources department.

Unplanned material is a natural, situational response. The material may be evolving and not following the expected business path. Unexpected material is published occasionally and is not in an organized manner, date and time. Unexpected advertising problems apply to legal problems, or whether the email being sent reflects the company and brand appropriately. If a company sends out a Tweet or Facebook post so hastily, it can use unnecessarily offensive words or wording that may marginalize certain customers. The key difference among scheduled and unexpected is acceptance of material. Marketing executives should still accept unexpected material much sooner. Industries can overlook mistakes because it is being rushed. While using unexpected material the marketing executive must be prepared to give a response and be able to react to the problems that can arise out of these.

Repercussions on Customary Advertising

1. Diminishing use: Traditional media methods involve print as well as TV advertisements. The Digital world has indeed replaced TV as the biggest advertising business. Websites often consist of the banner as well as pop-up advertisements. Social media sites do not always have advertisements. In return, goods have entire pages and are clever to communicate with customers. TV commercials sometimes conclude with a spokesman telling audiences to check out the brand website to learn. Although famous, print advertisements had QR codes on them. Such QR codes could be read by cell phones and computers, bringing visitors to the brand website. Marketing is starting to move audiences from the conventional channels to the digital ones.

Although mainstream media, including newspaper and television ads, is increasingly replaced by the emergence of digital marketing, there is a space for conventional marketing. For instance, for magazines, reader base over most of the decades have shown a decrease. Nevertheless, readership of publications is still extremely loyal to write-only outlets. Percent of newspapers audiences only interpret the paper in its printed form, rendering well-placed advertising valuable.

2. The leaks: Web and online social leakages are the problems traditional media faces. Video and printed advertisements are sometimes seeping out to the globe sooner than expected through the Internet. Social media sites cause such breaches to go public, and several users see them quicker. Current marketers also experience the time gap. As social gatherings arise and televised live, sometimes there is a delay from airings on the U.S. East Coast as well as on the West Coast. Social media platforms are now an event-related center for feedback and communication. It allows people viewing the event to know the result before screening. The 2011 Academy Awards demonstrated it. Spectators on the Atlantic Coast heard who received the awards based on comments by people watching online on the eastern coast on social media. Because audiences knew who won, most tuned out, and scores were smaller. All the publicity and advertising brought into the case was wasted because fans had no way of watching.

3. Mistakes: Online marketing helps companies to communicate with their clients. Organizations however, safeguard their data and carefully watch posts and complaints on the social networks we use. An organization's top three social networking events during the prior year involved staff revealing too much data in public forums, misuse or disclosure to sensitive information, and enhanced lawsuit coverage. Thanks to the interactive nature of the site, in some situations, a single customer error has shown devastating effects for organizations.

4. The morals: Ethics standards associated with traditional advertising could also be extended to social networks. But, with social networking being really private and global, there is another set of complexities and problems that surround moral online. Through social networking innovation, the marketing company no longer will have to focus exclusively on the traditional statistics and archetypes generated by TV and newspapers, but they can still get what audiences like to learn from marketers, how they communicate socially, and also what their needs and desires are. The general idea of becoming moral when labeling social media is to be truthful with both the campaign's goals, avoid false ads, be mindful of privacy and security requirements (which includes not using private information for the benefit of consumers), value the reputation of users in the shared online environment and claim credit for any errors or failures that occur from your product Many social media advertisers use Facebook as well as Myspace platforms to try driving traffic to the next site. When using social networking sites to spread the message to actually interested individuals is legal, most people are playing the system of auto-friend connecting systems and spam updates and newsletters. Nevertheless, social bookmarking sites have become wise to such activities and are essentially blocking criminals.

Furthermore, social media sites are becoming extremely conscious of their followers, collecting information from their audiences to communicate with them in different ways. Social-networking site like Facebook works internally on a social marketing program that allows advertisers to target customers with contextual ads on the massive amounts of information that people share to themselves on the Internet. This could be immoral or moral to some people. Many individuals may respond negatively since they assume warrantless spying. On either hand, certain people that love this function since their social media platform knows their preferences and give them ads relevant towards those interests. Customers enjoy networking with people with similar interests and preferences. People that choose to also have their Facebook profile published should be mindful that companies will take the information which attracts themselves so that they can give them content and ads to increase their sales. Executives engage in social media for partnerships and client engagement.

5. *Statements of the Websites:* It includes monitoring the number of clicks, leads and sales to a particular media network page. Google Analytics is indeed a free tool which displays social media users actions and other data such as profiles and system size. These and other advertising deals will help advertisers choose the effective social media and advertising campaigns.

6. *Investment information return:* The aim of any promotional work is to create sales. While social networking is a valuable communication tool, it is often hard to quantify its contribution to income. Return on Investment (ROI) can be calculated by contrasting advertising analytical quality with communication list or customer relationship management (CRM), and then linking marketing campaigns to revenue.

7. *Customer reaction:* Many consumers take to social networks to show appreciation or disappointment with products, brands, or services. Furthermore, advertisers will calculate how often consumers consider their product and how successful their SMM approaches are. During recent research, 72 percent of respondents said they received a reply to their Twitter grievances within an hour.

8. *Social media sports:* Social marketing in athletics has grown as sports teams with clubs understand the importance of maintaining social media relationships with their supporters as well as other viewers. After social marketing came into being, advisers and consumers have become wiser and more cautious about how they collect data and deliver ads. The involvement of data collection people no longer needs targeting specific markets. This is a broad legal gray area. It is a privacy violation for many people, there are no laws preventing these businesses from using the data on their websites.

Conclusion

The main goal of using social networks in advertising remains as a correspondence tool that forces companies available for those willing to engage in their good or service and makes them noticeable to those without understanding of their products. These businesses use social media to push buzz, learn from others and target clients. This is the only marketing technique which can finger customers for every level of product decision-making. Social media marketing has many other opportunities. It suggests that if companies were less or less involved in the internet, they usually appear less on Internet searches. While networks such as Facebook, Instagram, and Google+ provide a higher number of monthly active users, mobile systems based on facial offline caching, moreover, have gained a higher communication rate, recorded the fastest growth and transformed the way customers participate with product content. Facebook has a 1.46 percent communication rate with such a median of 130 million monthly active users as compared to Twitter. Like conventional media, sometimes price-prohibitive to many businesses a social media presence does not entail excessive financial planning.

Towards this end, businesses are using systems like Instagram, Facebook, Twitter and Snapchat to achieve viewers much deeper than using conventional print, TV/advertising outside at a fraction of the price, since most websites could be used at very little cost. These have transformed the way of businesses to view the customer experience. The significant percentage of customer relationships are being performed online platforms with a much higher exposure. Consumers now can post products and services evaluations, rate customer support, and actually ask business queries or express concerns via social networks. As per the Measuring progress, over 80 percent of customers use the internet to lookup products or services. Companies do use online marketing to construct trust relations with customers. Businesses may also hire staff to explicitly handle such social networking relationships, which typically disclose under title of online discussion executives. Managing these experiences satisfactorily, it could lead to increased customer loyalty. To this end and to correct a firm's view of the market, three steps are being taken to resolve customer issues, define the nature of online buzz, activate influencers to support, and build a reasonable response.

Chapter – 12

VISUAL MARKETING

Introduction

Visual marketing is the practice studying the interaction with an object, its meaning, and it is graphic. As a key element of modern advertising, digital marketing relies on researching and examining whether visuals can also be used to create the of artifacts center of visual marketing. Thus, the aim was that the brand as well as its visual interaction is deliberately connected and indistinguishable and their convergence is what hits consumers, attracts them and determines their preferences. Use picture and graphic dynamism will render a business plan more effective and unforgettable. When handled skillfully, photographs will transform ideas and abstract objects into something much more real, shaping the viewer's interpretation. These allow people see a product and its image in the mind, and understand when it comes to buying.

Interactive advertising can be a part of every component of the marketing process. Advertising tries to persuade customer purchasing behavior, and visual marketing improves that by recollection, awareness and personality influences.

Growing developments in the use of image-based websites with social media networks including Pinterest, Twitter, LinkedIn, Facebook's timeline app support users trying to believe what they see and thus, require for visual promotion.

Platforms of Visual Marketing

Digital advertising involves all digital indicators such as branding, posters, promotional devices, carriages, equipment, brochures, data CDs, and blogs, all that hits the limelight.

The origins of such understanding artifacts lie in Susan Sontag's article on "Camp," published in the 1960s; the author points out that things are not important by themselves but perhaps in the manner they are interpreted, arising from a number of factors that focus on the background of the artifact, its meaning, its appearance and perception in the beholder's eyes. As it evolved, graphical advertising emphasized the concealing of an item, instead of being a commodity, becomes the subject of its own making, thereby turning it from itself into something else, at the exact moment it enters the market. Things are: actual - as we see; recognizable - what they are created from; ideal - their classic identity; and interaction - with their connection to taste.

So, visual advertising takes attention away from conventional goals to concentrate on interest groups that are no more broken down by age, race, employment or any other state records and social settings but by form of participation, be it sporting, private artistic, etc. These classes include visual, auditory, voice, signal and structured symbols they use to interact. Therefore, the verbal team activities have been behind the new sub-alphabets which can be utilized to interpret direct mail strategies with the community itself.

One of individual motivating almost anthropological attitude is Marc Augé, who noted in his book *Le temps en ruines* that: "the world where image is omnipresent requires the reality to be reflected in its image". Paolo Schianchi's work underlined how well the idea of putting forward the picture of truth created of each identity group consists of vocabulary sets consisting of terms, sounds, pictures, tastes and forms which make different forum-alphabets when mixed separately. When decrypted correctly, these descriptive elements are the way to reach a collective and guide a response in it. This dimension of digital advertising creates highly targeted strategies which go right to the feelings and interpretations of truth of the consumers, using their own expressive linguistic.

The moralities, ontology and epistemology will be omitted from the images, and it is useless to inquire about anything good or bad, actual or imaginary, true or false, or what it implies. That is how the researchers invented the idea of symbolic expression at the root of graphical and oral post-alphabets, which relate to each person when they become part of the interest group. Digital advertising has incorporated these ideas and conveyed a brand to an audience which transcribes their psychological and human cultures, as we now know everybody lives. A dual existence, in each entity reflects him, being indivisible from either the unique person, as artifacts become his image. Digital advertising experts' project around all this and going from product layout to visual representation and thus building the aura around this one.

Virtual Engagement

Digital interaction is a measure to assess a company's degree of intimacy with its consumers. In the present social media culture, few things are important far more to advertisers as the strength of a client's emotions toward a certain company's brand or commodity. Marketing experts target clients and push them along the lead generation continuum to be consumers and supporters.

Virtual platforms play a key role in product system integration, where digital experiences have become the part of a marketing mix. All consumer operations take place in such a controlled setting, providing valuable feedback on interaction level. Consumer loyalty measure could be used to calculate how good an organization interacts with its society. It is a statistic, generated from integration of behavioral and statistical factors and is used in simulated reality events to determine lead performance.

Corporate experts have developed community involvement as a philosophy, as it became apparent that businesses need to concentrate on the actions of individual consumers or targets to assess the quality of the link they are able to develop.

Digital Marketing Communication

The advertising landscape as well as the consumer relationship platforms are changing quickly. Digital advertising is the latest update, among them. The digital world gives the company the ability to either succeed in their business or slip below ever-changing times. Facebook alone has billions monthly active users creating a virtual network where advertisers can interact and engage to consumers in ways that has never been. We can define their interests, customize their messages, and create alternative interactions and correspondence. According to study, word of mouth or brand marketing is very powerful and helpful to customers as it provides a virtual world in which they can interact with one another. We can tell each other about the firm's lived experience, positives and negative. The success of this is shown with Trip Advisor, which, based on user reviews, has become the first request for flight information and influencing travel operators industry both consciously and subconsciously.

Online network can be used by companies not only just to supports users. We can probably build digital customer groups and customer loyalty. What companies connect in the virtual environment becomes increasingly relevant as their product represents. Asking questions and coping with grievances rapidly is critical and a simple way to start digital advertising. Since these digital networks are very public, this makes how companies interact with customers a very sensitive thing, as a negative experience impacts not only the main customer, but everyone who wants to see it. A negative review and remark will significantly impact future income on organizations.

Customers seem to be more comfortable when visiting the online markets as they are in home comfort and security. We prefer to not be less conscious of the range of marketing strategies employed in the actual market. Advertisers seek this as decisions and are taken freer and more readily. Being placed into a digital sense (emailed to users) and being more successful because consumers are more comfortable when shopping and ready to make impulse transactions. The online model allows individuals to buy immediately, rather than go to the real shop. Any visible fee makes it easier for all users not to know the cash they just invested. Digital retailing is a simple memory full of stores and deals.

The online marketplace depends on brand images, implying the colors and how the item appears that differ from the real product. Such images were edited using Images to make them more consumer-friendly. This is a downside because customers still need to experience, view or sample the brand before reaching a purchase decision. Firms also strand the physical and digital market. Though the internet is gradually become the major marketing tool of online practical support.

The Usage of Social Networking Platforms

Marketers use the digital medium as a way to market to customers especially social networks, like Facebook, Instagram, Twitter, etc. Social networks allow to categorize users by allowing communities to enter, defining their desires. Companies have now a conscience and selected market targeting in which they now can focus their ads. Companies can use online interaction as a way of contacting customers and get reviews, customer analysis and involvement, as well as provide the information they may need before making a purchase. Such online interaction helps the customer to create a feeling of' friendship with the company since they are able to communicate and chat effortlessly with them, building confidence and brand loyalty. A further tactic a company uses through virtual environment is conducting games over social networks and taking full advantage of all its availability. Such contests are sometimes used to attract more supporters: "like and share this message". Through "like and share this message," companies are now becoming more innovative to maximize efficiency and profits. The promotion not just offered viewers a sensation of being a National Geographic artist, and also provided National Geographic a great deal of information regarding their clients and their transportation habits, image strategies and so much more.

Social networking was a groundbreaking business strategy for several businesses. Tourism, for example, previously regulated by travel companies and travel leaflets today controls social media sites and reservation sites. Tourism businesses have a simple forum to post pictures to encourage and draw customers. Give customers details on where and how to go out and the place to eat, and even when traveling by effective marketing campaigns could be used to protect the customer recall their experience there. Companies can choose either paid ads or free social networking advertising. Compensation is where the corporation pays the social networking site to display the ads on the customers' computer without the user's consent. These would be typically on either the display hand or "paid," based on about what the company costs. Paid as well as unpaid ads have equal impact on the desire of customers to buy other products.

Role of Organizations

Digital interaction is also new to industry, even though it is difficult to establish the returns on marketing spending in the virtual environment. Research indicates the impact of advertising on users, the results revealed that social media advertising is efficient, however when cross channel marketing is also used efficiently. Cross channel marketing occurs when a company promotes on multiple channels, such as social networks and publications. Scholars advise that executives choose to accept social networking as a way of further engaging with clients and helping to create a greater connection. This will boost customer loyalty and raise consumer demand. Guidelines recommend that management engage in digital advertising, but are cautious about the number, as the specific effects are still not entirely clear. It is known that social networking marketing is much more important to boost brand identity and build customer loyalty than revenue on a product. That is because the customer does not really need or want the actual product, yet they still have seen the label and become acquainted with anything.

Conclusion

Old marketing tactics is no longer appropriate for contemporary society, despite Internet age taking over, changing the direction of advertisers approach to customers. While advertising previously business concentrated on the item, it has become best to focus on the customer as well as the brand alone. Companies can't expect to interact as they were, where they either post photos including product features. They will update their advertising strategy to satisfy online consumer demands. Scholars bring up the question about whether companies ought to be able to publish on social networking sites, a way to reach peers and used as a means of leisure. In these sites, company ads can be seen as invasive, and invasions of privacy or even immoral. This might hurt the company's name. Hence, users usually accept the social networks as companies which need the support for their channels. But they agree that marketing is really the way networks are financed and embrace it as appropriate. So it does not mean that customers may not experience so repetitive and intrusive ads, which may in turn affect reciprocation to the advertisement or harm their product relation. Nonetheless, the question reminds companies that they must value the platforms as a venue of peer-to-peer discussions and personal recreation and guarantee that their participation in these platforms is not patronizing or invasive.

Chapter - 13

CUSTOMER DATA PLATFORM

Customer Data Platform (CDP) is indeed a form of bundled technology providing a continuous, centralized database open to many other programs. Clear and merge data from various sources to produce a single consumer account is important in data processing. According to the scholars, Gartner customer data platforms have grown from a variety of developing markets, like multi-channel community management, label strategic planning and information convergence.

Furthermore, several CDPs have additional functionality like brand quality analysis software, statistical engineering, and digital marketing.

Common features of CDPs: The common features of CDPs include controlled, integrated, continuous, common consumer information registry, identity as well as other data of any external source; clear identification that connect all customer information; available via sub processes and designed to meet marketers demands for community management, sales and marketing analytics.

It also provides a consumer perspective; divide consumers into customer sections; and allows users to anticipate the best next step with a product.

Data Collection

A major benefit of a CDP is its capacity to gather data from either a wide range of sources both online as well as offline, with such a variety of media and structures and turn it into a structured type. Several types of information a generic CDP can operate for involve.

It can provide Consumer activities such as searching, page or device behaviors, banner clicks, etc.

Relational information is collected from transactions, refunds, POS terminals results.

Consumer characteristics such as age, race, birth, first sales date, differentiation information, and forecasts Brand assessment data gathered perceptions, clicks, scope, interaction, etc.

Consumer company experience information from consumer-service transactions, NPS ratings, catboats info, etc.

Technologies of Marketing Automation

A CDP is significantly different from application development platforms in design, while CDPs provide one of the features of marketing platforms and customer experience channels. CDP devices speak to other programs. You maintain information that the communication or automated method does not. This is useful for evaluating patterns, analytics and advice that can exploit historical information.

CDP and DMP

Data Management Platform (DMP) stores electronic and confidential website data. CDPs gather information from an identified person. CDP clients may use information for more customized advertising and distribution.

Demonstration of DMP and CDPs

Manage individual customer information with a common account.

Manage customer groups with private accounts.

Sources of data Deal with both unidentified data (cookie, user IDs and IP address) and documented personal information (e.g.: addresses, identities, mail, telephone).

Function for anonymous data (cookies, user Identifiers, IP addresses).

Using advanced cleaning and balancing technologies that will provide heavy-quality integrated customer accounts.

Using probabilistic key mapping to map and create secret profiles through digital platforms.

Software upgrades system batch and flow software to maintain profiles up-to-date and reliable.

Upgrades consumer accounts after one or two days.

Information management Continues to maintain precious archives that remain across time.

Retains short-term confidential consumer information.

Conclusion

A database server or data center gathers data, typically from same origin and database system. Although this data can be systematically synthesized. No device method offers the identities solution required to integrate a single consumer experience. Data repositories are sometimes maintained at regular times, while CDPs integrate and provide actual-time data. Many CDPs using the same technology as database reservoirs in practice; the distinction is that the CDP has built-in functionality to do extra filtering and render it accessible, whereas a data pool might not.

Chapter – 14

CONCLUSION

Benefits and Drawbacks of Digital Marketing

The concept of digital marketing can be quite relevant in the general interaction between both the customer and the company. So, digital marketing will touch growing potential customers.

The benefit of online marketing is that customers are introduced to specifically marketed brand and item. Clarifying the commercial is easily accessible and can be viewed any time everywhere.

For digital marketing, though, this form of approach has drawbacks. Another major issue of digital marketing is, it is heavily Internet-dependent. This can also be called a drawback because web may not be available in some places or users might have slow Internet connectivity.

Besides being largely dependent on the Web for social media marketing, this is subject to all kinds of spam, and advertisers may find it difficult to differentiate their ads and get people to engage in conversation about an organization's brand identity or goods.

While digital marketing keeps increasing and expand, companies take real benefit of using software and the Web as an effective means of communication to their consumers to enable them to broaden the scope. There are risks which are not widely discussed owing to the business depends on it. Marketing companies will recognize both the benefits and drawbacks of online marketing while assessing their marketing plan and business objectives.

Some businesses can be unfairly viewed by users as some people lose internet confidence due to the volume of ads on websites that can be deemed spam. It can damage their reputation and credibility and disclose them as not reliable and unethical.

The drawback is that a person or small group of individuals will hurt a brand's identity. For example, Doppelgangers is a phrase used to approve of a brand identity shared by anti-brand protesters, writers, and opinion makers. Generally, product produces pictures that draw their consumers psychologically. Nevertheless, some would argue with this picture and change this photo to view it in a humorous or cynical way, thereby distorting the identity of the product, making a Lookalike picture, blog or material.

There are two key practical issues in online marketing. One is online advertising of particular product groups, implying that customer brand can be perpetuated across digital channels. Industrial materials and pharmaceuticals cannot be sold electronically. Second is, digital marketing simply distributes data to customers to whom, that have no purchase authority and power. And thus the representation of online marketing in actual sales size is skeptical. In modern digital business world with the potential to be interactive through various digital platforms, nation borders as well as cultural barriers, social networking has created a new communication tool. Online marketing is among the fastest-changing platform in marketing fields. The strategies used and established for digital marketing have originated a long track in recent years. This also generated huge possibilities for companies all over the world, but when you use online marketing for enterprise, there are some things you need to be mindful of.

Social networking is the latest real-time online advertising platform available in the world. Just like there are advertising benefits on this platform. Also, there are drawbacks to company owner and to the marketing company.so the management should be mindful to know and understand how it can affect the firm positively or negatively in all ways.

Merits of Digital Marketing

Some of the issues with reporting and describing a few of social networking marketing's total or specific benefits and drawbacks are that all of this depends on your company. A few of the main variances that you must be mindful of will affect the strengths and weaknesses are: through real-time interaction and networking, the digital marketing environment may have a lot of benefits and possibilities which could not be feasible or even conceivable earlier. Some of those are:

- Real-time consumer ads and reviews
- Digital real-time networking and revealing advertising or other online content
- Complimenting current network infrastructure such as portals, etc.
- Aimed network coverage you want
- Improved probability of free advertisement (mouth word, oral, digital)
- Improved traffic to a particular site through navigation as well as connection sharing
- Further effective reporting of your activities and promotions
- Opportunities for previously unknown cultures and market segments
- Socioeconomic coverage to existing and new market segments
- Complement the conventional digital advertising activities
- Compliment the conventional digital advertising activities

- Expanding general business opportunity and visibility
- Good Marketing and business connections
- Enhanced marketing research and evaluation

Online-Marketing Benefits

Broad demographic can be met cost effectively and measurably. Certain online marketing gains include growing customer loyalty, boosting sales online.

Global influence: a platform helps you to discover new opportunities and exchange for just a modest investment.

Low cost: a properly funded and very well-targeted online marketing strategy will attract the right consumers at much cheaper cost than conventional methods of advertising.

Traceable, tangible outcomes: Tracking your social media marketing through business intelligence as well as other online tools makes it much easier to evaluate how successful your strategy is. You can get comprehensive information of how consumers use the websites or react to ads.

Personalization: If your consumer list is connected to your page; you will welcome them with personalized deals whenever anyone enters the platform. The further you purchase, the more you should easily build your brand experience and sell with them.

Straight forwardness: By interacting and properly managing social networks, you can develop brand loyalty and establish a credibility for simple interaction.

Digital media: Digital marketing allows you to create entertaining ads utilizing marketing techniques. Such material (images, photos, articles) will acquire social currency, flowing from user to consumer, being viral.

Better exchange rates: If you have a blog, the clients are only a couple of taps away from buying. Unlike many other outlets that allow people to walk and call and then go to a store, digital marketing can also be smooth and instant.

Furthermore, all these elements of internet marketing will lead to more revenue.

1. It is quite cheap.
2. It has a large audience exposure.
3. In it multi-demographic caters together.
4. It is extremely fast.
5. Online marketing touches policy-makers.
6. Digital marketing produces twin-way product experiences.
7. It has the ability to improve customer care.
8. When done properly it can help get greater brand recognition rates.

Digital-Marketing Challenges

Many of the disadvantages and drawbacks of digital marketing which need to be mindful of include:

Competence and knowledge: It need to ensure that the employees have the necessary skills and knowledge for effective online marketing. Resources, technologies and patterns change quickly, and staying up-to-date is crucial.

Time consuming: The activities like designing digital advertising strategies as well as producing promotional material will take a long time. Test the returns to guarantee a yield-on-investment.

Strong rivalry: When you can hit a global communications advertising community, you always face intense competition. It may be a struggle to stick against rivals and draw attention amongst many digital product posts.

Grievances and reviews: You can see any negative comments or critique of your product through social networking sites and reviews platforms. Digital efficient customer support can be difficult. Negative feedback or inability to respond successfully will harm your product.

Security and safety concerns: There are many regulatory requirements to capture and use customer information for digital advertising purposes. Carefully abide with confidentiality and data privacy laws.

Drawbacks of Digital Marketing

As with all benefits that online marketing will offer something to your company, you have to be mindful of the pitfalls that will most likely affect your choices when it comes to beginning with marketing, your advertising campaigns and activities or stopping with your current social media impact.

1. It is time consuming.
2. Know how to manage negative media responses as they apply to you easily.
3. Gain control from your side.
4. It is difficult to calculate the ROI.

Actual-time customer reviews and comments Complaints from customers and feedback noticeable and available for public review. Strategic use of business and personal capital and monitor the digital media campaign. Experience and expertise required to maximize the online footprint. Social networking and the field of browsers keep changing and grow and give users the best choices, so the approach might not be in stone for a number of years, and some of the biggest social media marketing techniques are those that can and are tracked and continuously updated to changes in the market and patterns. Further the marketing can be tracked; the more flexible the strategy is to developments in your target audience and related social media platforms.

Conclusion

The benefit in online marketing is that it is so broad that there were no restrictions on its regional scope. It allows businesses to be global and extend their market scope in areas apart from their home country.

When previously mentioned, digital technology gives consumers 24/7 delivery as well as allowing customers to buy online at a certain hour of the day or night, not only when stores are over and around the globe. It is a great advantage for merchants to do this and lead customers directly to their web store. This has also offered an opportunity for businesses to be solely based digital, instead of have a website or shop due to online marketing's success and capability.

Another benefit is that online marketing is very easy to calculate, allowing marketers to know the extent of their ads, whether digital marketing succeeds or not, and the level of interaction and discussion included.

Brands use Digital space to meet their potential customers; online marketing has become a lucrative career choice. Today, businesses are more likely to hire recognizable persons to execute digital advertising techniques, and that has led the channel becoming a preferred option for individuals encouraging organizations to step up and give qualified Digital Marketing courses.

A downside to online advertising is the vast number of alternative products and services that use the same online marketing techniques. For instance, when someone looks for a brand or a particular product online, whenever a related company uses focused online ads then they can show on the client's home page, encouraging the consumer to check for alternative choices for a lower price or higher quality with the same brand or a faster place to find whatever they are interested in online.

REFERENCES

McCole, Patrick (2004). "Refocusing marketing to reflect practice". *Marketing Intelligence & Planning.* 22 (5): 531–539.

Luo, Margaret Meiling; Chen, Ja-Shen; Ching, Russell K.H; Liu, Chu-Chi (2011). "An examination of the effects of virtual experiential marketing on online customer intentions and loyalty". *The Service Industries Journal.* 31.

Gilmore, James H; Pine, B. Joseph (2002). "Customer experience places: The new offering frontier". *Strategy & Leadership.* 30 (4): 4.

eMarketer (25 September 2013), Worldwide Ad Growth Buoyed by Digital, Mobile Adoption, eMarketer, archived from the original on 12 November 2013

"Digital Marketing Communication". *International Chamber of Commerce.* Retrieved 12 September 2017.

Nielsen (20 January 2016). "Connected Commerce is Creating Buyers Without Borders". *Nielsen Global. Nielsen Global.* Retrieved 24 March 2016.

Kumar, A.; Bezawada, R.; Rishika, R.; Janakiraman, R.; Kannan, P. K. (2016). "From Social to Sale: The Effects of Firm-Generated Content in Social Media on Customer Behavior". *Journal of Marketing.* 80 (1): 7–25.

Van Niekerk, A (2007). "Strategic management of media assets for optimizing market communication strategies, obtaining a sustainable competitive advantage and maximizing return on investment: An empirical study". *Journal of Digital Asset Management*. 3 (2): 89–98.

Hudson, S., Huang, L., Roth, M. S., & Madden, T. J. (2016). "The influence of social media interactions on consumer–brand relationships: A three-country study of brand perceptions and marketing behaviors". *International Journal of Research in Marketing*, 3327–41.

World Economics (June 2015). "Digital and Mobile Continues to Dominate Share of Marketing Budgets". 10 January 2018.

Whiteside, S (January 2016). "Five digital marketing lessons from comScore". Warc.com. Retrieved 10 January 2018.

Square2Marketing (2012). "Online advertising: Google AdWords & pay-per-click". YouTube. Retrieved 10 January 2018.

Pratik Dholakiya (14 April 2015). "3 Digital Marketing Channels That Work for Every Advertiser". *Entrepreneur*. Retrieved 17 October 2015.

Dapko, J. L.; Artis, A. B. (2014). "Less is More: An Exploratory Analysis of Optimal Visual Appeal and Linguistic Style Combinations in a Salesperson's Initial-Contact E-mail to Millennial Buyers Within Marketing Channels". *Journal of Marketing Channels*. 21 (4): 254–267."IAB internet advertising revenue report: 2012 full year results" (PDF). PricewaterhouseCoopers, *Internet Advertising Bureau*. April 2013.

Drell, Lauren (26 April 2011). "4 Ways Behavioral Targeting is Changing the Web". Mashable.com.

Moe, Wendy W. (2013). "Chapter 9: Targeting Display Advertising" (PDF). *Advanced Database Marketing: Innovative Methodologies & Applications for Managing Customer Relationships*. Gower Publishing, London. ISBN 978-1409444619.

Tulloch, Mitch (2003). Koch, Jeff; Haynes, Sandra (eds.). Microsoft Encyclopedia of Security. Redmond, Washington: Microsoft Press. p. 16. ISBN 978-0-7356-1877-0.

Suzanne Vranica; Mike Shields (23 September 2016). "Doubts About Digital Ads Rise Over New Revelations". *Wall Street Journal*. Dow Jones & Company, Inc. Retrieved 25 September 2016.

"Marketers Focus on Making Attribution Data Actionable: Industry experts discuss real-time optimisation of cross-platform attribution findings". *emarketer.com*. Retrieved 7 September 2015.

Moses, Lucia (2 April 2013). "The New York Times Tries Another Interactive Ad Unit: This time, for Prudential. *Adweek*.

Brian, Matt (22 May 2013). "Twitter steps into interactive ads, lets users sign up for offers directly from their timeline. The Verge. "Measuring the effectiveness of online advertising" (PDF). pwc.com. PricewaterhouseCoopers France, IAB France, *Syndicat des Regies Internet*. 2010. p. 8. Archived from the original (PDF) on 16 June 2013.

"Revenue Outcomes Matter to Online Advertisers: Advanced Automation Can Improve Efficiency And Results" (PDF). *marinsoftware.com*. Forrester Consulting. January 2013.

Lee, Joowon; Ahn, Jae-Hyeon (2012). "Attention to Banner Ads And Their Effectiveness: An Eye-Tracking Approach". *International Journal of Electronic Commerce*. 17 (1): 119–137.

Clifford, Stephanie (29 September 2009). "Two-Thirds of Americans Object to Online Tracking". Retrieved 20 June 2013.

Heusssner, Ki Mae (13 February 2013). "Divorcees, Southerners Most Concerned About Web Privacy: 90 percent of online adults worry about privacy online, study shows".

"2012 Internet Crime Report" (PDF). Internet Crime Complaint Center. FBI and National White Collar Crime Center. 2013

Rosenberg, Eric (31 March 2007). "U.S. Internet fraud at all-time high: 'Nigerian' scam and other crimes cost $198.4 million". *San Francisco Chronicle*.

Mlot, Stephanie (1 February 2013). "Online Advertising More Likely to Spread Malware Than Porn". *PC Magazine*. Retrieved 16 June 2013.

"Cisco 2013 Annual Security Report" (PDF). Cisco. 2013. Archived from the original (PDF) on 28 February 2013. Retrieved 16 June 2013.

"CryptoWall! crooks! 'turn! to! Yahoo! ads! to! spread! ransomware!". *The Register*. 11 August 2014. Retrieved 4 January 2015.

Special Advertising Problems: Internet Advertising: Unique Issues Posed by the Internet. *The Law of Advertising*. 56.06. Matthew Bender & Co, Inc. 2013.

"Self-Regulatory Principles for Online Behavioral Advertising" (PDF). *iab.net*. Interactive Advertising Bureau. 1 July 2009.

"Europe's Online Advertising Industry Releases Self-Regulation Framework". iabeurope.eu. 11 April 2011. Archived from the original on 17 April 2011.

Singel, Ryan (8 July 2009). "Internet Ad Industry Begs for Regulation". *Wired*. Retrieved 12 June 2013.

"FTC Strengthens Kids' Privacy, Gives Parents Greater Control Over Their Information By Amending Children's Online Privacy Protection Rule". *Federal Trade Commission*. 19 December 2012.

"Performance & Accountability Report, Fiscal Year 2012" (PDF). Federal Trade Commission. 2012. p. 6.

Jansen, B. J. (2011). *Understanding Sponsored Search: Coverage of the Core Elements of Keyword Advertising.* Cambridge University Press: Cambridge, UK.

Stefanie Olsen and Gwendolyn Mariano (April 5, 2002). "Overture sues Google over search patent". *CNET.*

Yahoo! Inc. (2002). "Yahoo! and Overture Extend Pay-for-Performance Search Agreement". *Yahoo! Press Release.* Retrieved May 18, 2010.

Shaltoni, AM (2016-07-01). "E-marketing education in transition: An analysis of international courses and programs". *The International Journal of Management Education.* 14 (2): 212–218. doi:10.1016/j.ijme.2016.04.004. ISSN 1472-8117.

Zhang, M., Jansen, B. J., and Chowdhury, A. (2011) "Influence of Business Engagement in Online Word-of-mouth Communication on Twitter: A Path Analysis. Electronic Markets". *The International Journal on Networked Business.* 21(3), 161–175.

Evans, Dave (16 September 2010). *Social Media Marketing: The Next Generation of Business Engagement.* John Wiley & Sons. pp. 15–. ISBN 978-0-470-94421-9. Retrieved 28 July 2013.

Schaffer, Neal. *Maximize Your Social: A One-Stop Guide to Building a Social Media Strategy for Marketing and Business Success.* Somerset, NJ, USA: John Wiley & Sons, 2013. ProQuest ebrary. Web. 3 December 2014. Copyright © 2013. John Wiley & Sons. All rights reserved.

Bergström, Thamwika (2013). *Marketing and PR in Social Media: How the utilization of Instagram builds and maintains customer relationships (PDF).* Stockholm University. p. 5.

Schaefer, Kayleen (20 May 2015). "Social media is a massive construct. And, there is an amalgam of personalities online". *Harper's Bazaar.*

Deis, Michael H.; Kyle Hensel (2010). "Using social media to increase advertising and improve marketing". Entrepreneurial Executive: p.87.

Chiang, I-Ping; Chung-Hsien Hsieh (October 2011). "Exploring the impact of blog marketing on consumers". *Social Behavior and Personality*. 39 (9): 1245–1250.

Muntinga, Daniel; Moorman, M.; Smit, E. (2011). "Introducing COBRAs exploring motivations for brand-related social media use". *International Journal of Advertising*. 30 (1): 13–46. doi:10.2501/IJA-30-1-013-046.

Schivinski, Bruno; Christodoulides, George; Dabrowski, Dariusz (2016-03-01). "Measuring Consumers' Engagement With Brand-Related Social-Media Content". *Journal of Advertising Research*. 56 (1): 64–80. doi:10.2501/JAR-2016-004. ISSN 0021-8499.

Kim, Ellen; Mattila, A.; Baloglu, S. (2011). "Effects of gender and expertise on consumers' motivation to read online hotel reviews". *Cornell Hospitality Quarterly*. 52 (4): 399–406.

"Navigating Regulatory Challenges in Analytics, Data Science and AI" (PDF). *Sia Partners*. Retrieved March 27, 2019.

Jansen, Jim (July 2011). *Understanding Sponsored Search: Core Elements of Keyword Advertising*. New York, NY, USA: Cambridge University Press. p. 44. ISBN 9781107011977.

Broder, Andrei (Fall 2002). "A Taxonomy of Web Search" (PDF). *SIGIR Forum*. 36 (2): 5–6. Retrieved 27 December 2016.

"Definition of digital marketing". *Financial Times*. Archived from the original on 29 November 2017. Retrieved 22 August 2015.

"Domains of Digital Marketing Channels in the Sharing Economy". *Journal of Marketing Channels*.

Heikki, Karjaluoto. "The usage of digital marketing channels in SMEs". *Journal of Small Business and Enterprise Development.* 22 (4): 633–651.

Nielsen (20 January 2016). "Connected Commerce is Creating Buyers Without Border". *Nielsen Global. Nielsen Global.* Retrieved March 25, 2016.

Dahlen, Micael (2010). *Marketing Communications: A Brand Narrative Approach.* Chichester, West Sussex UK: John Wiley & Sons Ltd. p. 36.

Schoenbachler, Denise D.; Gordon, Geoffrey L.; Foley, Dawn; Spellman, Linda (1997). "Understanding consumer database marketing". *Journal of Consumer Marketing.* 15 (1): 5–19.

Clark, Dorie (11 November 2012). "The End of the Expert: Why No One in Marketing Knows What They're Doing," *Forbes*, archived from the original on 4 November 2013.

McCambley, Joe (2013-12-12). "The first ever banner ad: why did it work so well?". *The Guardian..* Retrieved 14 March 2018.

Brinkley, Claire (18 October 2012). "Digital marketing is growing in Australia, but so is the skills gap". *Econsultancy*, archived from the original on 21 October 2012

"Digital Marketing Communication". *International Chamber of Commerce.* Retrieved 12 September 2017.

Nielsen (3 February 2016). "What Are Connected Shoppers Doing and Not Doing Online". *Nielsen Global. Nielsen Global.* Retrieved 24 March 2016.

Nielsen (20 January 2016). "Connected Commerce is Creating Buyers Without Borders". *Nielsen Global. Nielsen Global.* Retrieved 24 March 2016.

Tiago, Maria Teresa Pinheiro Melo Borges; Veríssimo, José Manuel Cristóvão (2014). "Digital Marketing and Social Media; Why Bother?". *INBAM*, Business Horizons.

"EBSCO Publishing Service Selection Page". *Eds.a.ebscohost.com*. Retrieved 10 January 2018.

Holmberg, C et al. (2016). "Adolescents' presentation of food in social media: An explorative study". *Appetite*. doi:10.1016/j.appet.2016.01.009. 1;99:121–129. PMID 26792765.

Nielsen (17 December 2015). "Tops of 2015: Digital". *Nielsen Insights Media and Entertainment*. Nielsen.

Sakas, D. P., Dimitrios, N. K., & Kavoura, A. (2015). "The Development of Facebook's Competitive Advantage for Brand Awareness. Procedia Economics And Finance", 24 (*International Conference on Applied Economics (ICOAE) 2015, 2–4 July 2015, Kazan, Russia*), 589–597.

Kumar, A.; Bezawada, R.; Rishika, R.; Janakiraman, R.; Kannan, P. K. (2016). "From Social to Sale: The Effects of Firm-Generated Content in Social Media on Customer Behavior". *Journal of Marketing*. 80 (1): 7–25.

Van Niekerk, A (2007). "Strategic management of media assets for optimizing market communication strategies, obtaining a sustainable competitive advantage and maximizing return on investment: An empirical study". *Journal of Digital Asset Management*. 3 (2): 89–98.

Hudson, S., Huang, L., Roth, M. S., & Madden, T. J. (2016). "The influence of social media interactions on consumer–brand relationships: A three-country study of brand perceptions and marketing behaviors". *International Journal of Research in Marketing*, 3327–41.

Gibbs, Samuel (18 September 2015). "Facebook's new opt-out for tracking ads is not enough, says privacy expert". *The Guardian – via The Guardian*.

Kim, Angella J.; Johnson, Kim K.P. (2016). "Power of consumers using social media: Examining the influences of brand-related user-generated content on Facebook". *Computers in Human Behavior.* 58: 98–108.

Pratik Dholakiya (14 April 2015). "3 Digital Marketing Channels That Work for Every Advertiser". *Entrepreneur.* Retrieved 17 October 2015.

Terlutter, R.; Capella, M. L. (2013). "The Gamification of Advertising: Analysis and Research Directions of In-Game Advertising, Advergames, and Advertising in Social Network Games". *Journal of Advertising.* 42 (2/3): 95–112.

Li, H.; Lo, H. (2015). "Do You Recognize Its Brand? The Effectiveness of Online In-Stream Video Advertisements". *Journal of Advertising.* 44 (3): 208–218.

Schiele, Kristen; Chen, Steven (2018-03-26). "Design Thinking and Digital Marketing Skills in Marketing Education: A Module on Building Mobile Applications". *Marketing Education Review.* 28 (3): 150–154. doi:10.1080/10528008.2018.1448283. ISSN 1052–8008.

Staton, Mark G. (2015-12-07). "Improving Student Job Placement and Assessment Through the Use of Digital Marketing Certification Programs". *Marketing Education Review.* 26 (1): 20–24. doi:10.1080/10528008.2015.1091665. ISSN 1052–8008.

Liu, Xia; Burns, Alvin C. (2018-01-02). "Designing a Marketing Analytics Course for the Digital Age". *Marketing Education Review.* 28 (1): 28–40. doi:10.1080/10528008.2017.1421049. ISSN 1052–8008.

"Facebook.com Traffic, Demographics and Competitors – Alexa". www.alexa.com.

"Facebook Reports Third Quarter 2019 Results". investor.fb.com.

"Our History". Facebook. Retrieved November 7, 2018.

www.ingramcontent.com/pod-product-compliance
Lightning Source LLC
Chambersburg PA
CBHW030759180526
45163CB00003B/1086